# HOME OF THE GREAT PECAN

# GREAT PECAN

*Stephen Bittrich*

**BROADWAY PLAY PUBLISHING INC**
224 E 62nd St, NY NY 10065-8201
212 772-8334 fax: 212 772-8358
BroadwayPlayPub.com

HOME OF THE GREAT PECAN
© Copyright 2016 by Stephen Bittrich

First printing: January 2016
I S B N: 978-0-88145-638-7

Cover art: Phillip De Vita
Book design: Marie Donovan
Page make-up: Adobe Indesign
Typeface: Palatino
Printed and bound in the U S A

HOME OF THE GREAT PECAN began as a stand-alone 10-minute play entitled BRAIN SUCKING (the first scene of the full-length play), was produced by Actor's Theatre of Louisville, and was subsequently published in *Dramatics Magazine*.

The play was first presented using the 4 person format by Panties Optional Productions (Producers, Colleen Cosgrove and Mary Louise Picerno; Production Advisor, Hamilton Clancy) in November 2001. It was performed on the second floor space of 78th Street Theater Lab with the following cast and creative contributors:

GREELEY GREEN *(Actor G roles)* .................. Max Björquist
ED *(Actor E roles)* ....................................Jimi Egan
TAMMIE LYNN SCHNEIDER
*(Actor T roles)*.......................................... Colleen Cosgrove
ROSY FAY STADTMUELLER
*(Actor R roles)* ..................................... Maria Ryan

*Director*...................................................... Shelley Delaney
*Lighting design* ...............................Deborah Constantine
*Set design* ................................................Jeremy C Douchette
*Costume design*............................................ Deborah Caney
*Sound design*.............................. Christopher A Granger/
                                                        Granger Musicwerks
*Sound engineer* .................................................Asa Wember
*Graphic design* ........................................................ Paula Ng

*Special thanks to Shelley Delaney who was not credited as a dramaturg, but offered enormous help in that capacity.*

The world premiere of HOME OF THE GREAT
PECAN was presented by The Drilling Company
(Hamilton Clancy, Producing Artistic Director) in
January 2011 at The Drilling Company Theatre at 236
W 78th St, New York, with the following cast and
creative contributors:

REVEREND PAT.....................................................Scott Baker
MRS BART & LES GLENEHINKEL....................... Jarad Benn
BILLY POMGRANITE & OREST STELMACH (voices)
................................................................. Stephen Bittrich
MRS ROTTWEILER................................. Victoria Campbell
JOHNNY JOHNS (voice)........................... Hamilton Clancy
SONJA GUAREZ ............................................. Veronica Cruz
KITTY ST CLAIRE..................................... Anwen Darcy
FRANCIO ...................................................... Roberto Defelice
PRISCILLA ROTTWEILER ............................Amanda Dillard
ROSY FAY STADTMUELLER ...................... Amanda C Fuller
TAMMIE LYNN SCHNEIDER ............ Jessi Blue Gormezano
SHERIFF BART.......................................................Bill Green
GREELEY GREEN................................................David Marantz
CHUCKY CONNORS & DEKE ROTTWEILER. Brandon Reilly
DEPUTY DIGGITY.......................................... Steve Sherman
ED................................................................Dan Teachout

Director................................................... Hamilton Clancy
Lighting............................................ Miriam Nilofa Crowe
Sets...............................................................Jen Varbalow
Music ......................... Candee Land and David Marantz
Sound ......................................................... Alan B Smithee
Stage managers ............Ashley Scoles, Heather Cambanes
Graphic design ...............................................Phillip DeVita
Photography........................................................Lee Wexler

# CHARACTERS

*(In order of appearance)*

JOHNNY JOHNS *(voice only), the D J at the local radio station.*

GREELEY GREEN, *a good old Texas boy doing his best to avoid getting married.*

ED, GREELEY'S *laconic best friend who has an unexpected secret.*

TAMMIE LYNN SCHNEIDER, GREELEY'S *fiancée, a woman on the verge of a breakdown.*

ROSY STADTMUELLER, TAMMIE'S *gossipy church mouse friend who happens to be having an affair with* REVEREND PAT.

SHERIFF BART, *Seguin's no-nonsense sheriff who dispenses small town southern justice.*

DEPUTY DIGGITY, SHERIFF BART'S *overzealous and excitable new deputy.*

REVEREND PAT, *a very charismatic minister who happens to be embezzling money from his church.*

PRISCILLA ROTTWEILER, *a local beauty vying for the coveted title of Pecan Queen.*

MRS ROTTWEILER, PRISCILLA'S *overindulgent mother.*

DEKE ROTTWEILER, PRISCILLA'S *pesky little brother.*

CHUCKY CONNORS, *the town juvenile delinquent.*

BILLY POMGRANITE *(voice only), a local pecan grower.*

SONJA GUAREZ, *the owner of the local beauty parlor and* TAMMIE's *employer.*

FRANCIO, *an effeminate misfit with a heart of gold.*

MRS BART, *the gossipy wife of* SHERIFF BART *and a regular customer at Sonja's Beauty Parlor.*

OREST STELMACH *(voice only), a professor.*

LES GLENEHINKEL, *the chauvinistic owner of the local hardware store.*

KITTY ST CLAIR *(on video only), a local newscaster.*

# A NOTE CONCERNING THE NUMBER OF ACTORS

This play may be done by as few as 4 or as many as 19 actors.

If you are performing the 4 actor version, then use the "Four Actor Version" of the last scene.

If performing the (up to) 19 actor version, you need to use the "Large Cast Version" of the final scene (which is tacked on the end of this publication).

In a workshop of the play performed in New York City, we used 16 actors and doubled up the 3 other parts. There are many possibilities and variations for doubling actors. For example, we had the actor playing Les also play Mrs Bart (in drag). We had the actor playing Chucky also do the small voice-only part of Deke. There are a few roles which are voices on tape. These could be doubled with actors performing live.

One further note on the 4 person version: the four core characters are Greeley, Ed, Tammie, and Rosy, and thus the other various characters will be noted to belong to Actors G, E, T, and R, respectively. Therefore, when a new character is introduced, the indication of the actor meant to play him will follow. For example, Reverend Pat (Played by Actor E) would be the same actor playing Ed.

Dedicated to Seguin, Texas, where I grew up.

# ACT ONE

## Prelude

### 'Tis The Season

*(Before the curtain: at the proper time when all audience members have been seated, a song will precede the following voice over, signaling the official start of the play.)*

*(NOTE: Candee Land's version of "Strength of My Weakness" before the house lights go down and a sampling of her version of "Cowboy" fading into crickets after the opening radio announcement from* JOHNNY JOHNS *are good choices. Candee Land, who is a real performer from Seguin, Texas, can be substituted with a fictional name if need be.)*

JOHNNY JOHNS: *(V O)* Hey Folks, this is Johnny Johns over at K-W-A-D radio. It's a beautiful, warm October night, and you've been listening to the golden voice of Seguin's own [Candee Land] ...a homegrown sensation. We're as proud as can be to claim her as our own. Speakin' of homegrown sensations, it's about that time of year, folks. They're startin' ta fall off the trees like hail stones 'bout now, and that can only mean one thing, the Hunderd and Second Annual Pecan Festival, culminating in the crowning of the lucky Pecan Queen. So get on out there and getchu a bucket full of those tasty morsels...cuz after this next song, Aileen Rottweiler's gonna come on the air and share with y'all a family secret passed down through three generations...her blue ribbon winnin' pecan pie recipe. Mmmmmm, boy! Might wanna getchu a pen and paper while I play this next song...

*(More Texas music begins and then fades into...crickets.)*

## Scene 1

## Brain Sucking

*(Setting: The year is 1983. The place is Seguin, Texas, a small town...not so small that everyone knows each other's business, but small enough so that it sometimes feels that way. A clear, warm Saturday night on a large back porch out in the country.)*

*(At rise: The crickets chirp audibly. ED [Actor E] and GREELEY [Actor G], real Texas men who know how to relax, take in the star-lit night and experience the crickets. After a bit of "experiencing," GREELEY speaks—)*

GREELEY: Ed?

ED: Yeah, Greeley.

GREELEY: Crickets sure are perky tonight.

ED: Yep.

*(Pause. Crickets chirp.)*

GREELEY: Ed?

ED: Yeah, Greeley.

GREELEY: Whatta you spose those crickets are talkin' about?

*(ED listens.)*

ED: Mostly cricket matters, I guess.

GREELEY: Yep.

*(Crickets)*

GREELEY: Ed? *(Beat)* Ever had yer brain sucked out through yer nose?

ED: *(After a beat)* Nope.

GREELEY: Messy prospect.

*(The crickets chirp.)*

GREELEY: I'm not myself tonight, Ed.

ED: The *frijoles?*

GREELEY: Tammie saw this flying saucer land over't her field the other night.

ED: I heard.

GREELEY: Most folks are saying since her husband left in '78 she's been a little off.

ED: Yep.

GREELEY: They don't put much credence in the flying saucer thang. *(Beat)* But it's true, Ed.

*(Special vocal attention should be given to the alien word, "Yah".)*

GREELEY: I come from the planet *Yah*, twenty million, million earth miles away. My planet is warm and moist, and a zillion species of plant exist throughout our world. We, my species, are partly plants ourselves—Pod People. We sleep just below the dank soil by night and bask in the life-giving sun by day. Our sun-star is our god, but, according to mythology, our sun is doomed to explode and evaporate our planet in the *Yah* Year twenty-twenty-two—this earth year. Our scientists have confirmed this legend, so we have searched the galaxies far and wide for a new god. We have arrived on your planet, and now we worship your sun. In order to integrate ourselves into your society, we inhabit your earth bodies by attaching our pods to your faces and entering your brain cavities through the nose. Our eventual aim is the total annihilation of your species. Then we will readjust the orbit of earth to create a more tropical climate.

ED: *(After a beat)* You fart?

GREELEY: The beans.

ED: Damn. Potent som-bitch.

*(Crickets)*

GREELEY: "Why Seguin, Texas?" you may ask. Little too dry for our pods, you might thank. After careful scientific observation, our *Yah*-ian fleet was directed to Acapulco, Mexico, because it was concluded to possess the tropical climate which we are most comfortable in…but I had saucer failure over Dallas and had to make a crash landing here.

*(Crickets)*

GREELEY: As is well known, last month, the one called Greeley, the one which I now am, became engaged to be married to this Tammie Lynn Schneider.

ED: Yep. Clipped the picture outta the *Gazette*.

GREELEY: This Greeley, however, still has not come up with the two thousand to buy the long anticipated 14-carat/gold/diamond/ruby ring over't Dietz's Diamonds yet.

ED: Emma Dietz says she's expectin' it.

GREELEY: As is also well known, the long awaited, often spoke of "ring presenting fanfare" was to take place on the Corral Dance floor last night, "Frijole Friday," after a well publicized "surprise" announcement from the celebrated local country sensation, Candee Land of Candy Land and the Goolaks.

ED: Yep.

GREELEY: That tragic Friday night, when this one, Greeley, arrived at Tammie Schneider's place out on One-twenty-three Bypass, he first stopped into her greenhouse out back the house where I, the Pod Pers—

ED: Why?

GREELEY: Huh?

ED: Why'd he go back there first?

GREELEY: Uh...to check the Rhododendrons he gave her.

ED: Okay, I'll buy it.

GREELEY: There, sleeping among the ivy and the ferns, was I, the Pod Person. Greeley, a well-known plant enthusiast and long time employee of Norma Green's Thumb, caught me out of the corner of his eye and gasped at the sight of my glorious red and violet leaves. Being an inquisitive rascal, and despite having seen *Alien* five times at the Dixie Drive-In, he scooched up close to my pod to get a better look. I could smell his squishy, warm brains, and before he could cry out, I grappled my thorny vines on to his face.

ED: Thorny?

GREELEY: Sticky? Gooey.

ED: Gooey.

GREELEY: Of course, he missed his date that night without a word. My incubation period takes a full eight hours. For a full eight hours this one—Greeley— blindly wandered the dull, black Texas night as the pod attached to his face slowly sucked out his brains.

ED: Surprised it took a full eight.

GREELEY: At four o'clock in the morning the transformation was complete. The spent and wrinkled pod-shell dropped off, and *I* was ready to experience this new world and sample human pleasures.

ED: First stop: Seven-Eleven.

GREELEY: For a Slurpy and a six pack of Lone Star. Much to my surprise, the check out girl, Wendy, was friendly. She knew this Greeley. Knew him well. Well enough to let him cop a feel back in the video game room—right between Pac Man and Altered Beast.

ED: I love Pac Man.

GREELEY: This encounter with human delights was inadvertently observed by the Seven-Eleven manager, Miss Nosy Rosy Stadtmueller, who made an unannounced and previously unprecedented after hours visit to tabulate the register receipts.

ED: Yep. I heard.

GREELEY: *(After a beat, sadly)* This gossipy, nosy society is not understood by we *Yah*-ians.

ED: Welcome to Texas, Bud.

GREELEY: It's not this Greeley's fault. What *was* Greeley is now digested and only a shadow of him remains. Petty human emotions hold no importance for we *Yah*-ians.

ED: Ate his whole damn brain, huh?

GREELEY: That's the only way to occupy the host.

ED: Now, can you suck out other brains? Or are you limited to one brain per Pod Person?

GREELEY: You mean, could I come over there, as I am-- pod-less--pod-free--as it were, and suck out yer brain?

ED: Yep.

GREELEY: Yes, I could.

ED: So it's an all you can eat type deal.

GREELEY: Well, if say I found a more inviting host, I could switch, but then I'd have to exit the former body which would shrivel up and wither away--just as my pod did.

ED: Makes sense.

GREELEY: But that would be such a terrible waste of male virility.

*(ED and GREELEY guffaw. Crickets. GREELEY turns reflective.)*

GREELEY: Shoot...crickets have it easy, Ed.

ED: Yep.

GREELEY: *(After a beat)* Think she'll buy it?

ED: Not a snowball's chance in hell, Greeley.

*(Blackout. End of scene)*

## Scene Two

## Rag Session

*(Setting: The same Saturday night. The spacious back porch of* TAMMIE LYNN SCHNEIDER's *country house on 123 Bypass in Seguin, Texas.)*

*(At rise: As the scene begins, those same harmless little crickets are chirping—even more loudly—along with a few mutant bullfrogs.* TAMMIE *[Actor T] and* ROSY *[Actor R], Texas women on the edge, attempt to take in the star-lit night. Finally after a few moments of "experiencing,"* TAMMIE *nearly jumps out of her skin and runs to the edge of the porch—)*

TAMMIE: SHUT UP! JUST SHUT THE HELL UP!!!

*(The crickets and frogs suddenly stop.* TAMMIE *goes to sit back down, but before she's even completely in her seat, the crickets start up again—at about half volume.)*

TAMMIE: Goddamned crickets! Goddamned crickets!

ROSY: Tammie Lynn!

TAMMIE: What?

ROSY: Don't take the Lord's name in vain.

TAMMIE: Oh. Sorry, Lord.

*(Crickets.* TAMMIE *sobs out loud.)*

TAMMIE: *(At first sentimental)* Greeley...Greeley—
*(Then—)* Dickless son-of-a-bitch!

ROSY: Tammie!

TAMMIE: Or he will be when I get a holt ta him next.

ROSY: Well, if you ask me, he ain't worth it.

TAMMIE: Well, I guess I ain't asked you.

ROSY: Some thanks.

TAMMIE: If you hadn'ta butt your nose inta Seven
Eleven that late at night, none of this woulda
happened.

ROSY: That's right. Shoot the messenger.

TAMMIE: Miss Nosy.

ROSY: I just do it for you. I hate to see how he hurts
you.

TAMMIE: That's my business.

ROSY: I guess I'll jes' keep to myself next time.

TAMMIE: That'd be best.

ROSY: Just turn a blind eye *every time* he steps out on
you.

TAMMIE: I'd prefer that.

ROSY: All right.

*(Beat. Crickets)*

TAMMIE: Whadda you mean *"every time"*?

ROSY: *(Innocently)* What?

TAMMIE: Whadda you mean by sayin' *"every time he steps out on you"?*

ROSY: Nothing...or should I say *"nada"*.

TAMMIE: *Nada?*

ROSY: That's Spanish for "nothing".

TAMMIE: I know what it's Spanish for, Rosy, my momma didn't raise no dumb ass. Why'd you say *nada?*

ROSY: *No lo se.*

TAMMIE: I'm about to kick yer butt.

ROSY: You said you didn't wanna know *nada* about *nothing*. Every time I open my mouth I just get chewed out. Why should I say anything at all?

TAMMIE: *Puta! Pendejo!*

ROSY: I *know* what that means, Tammie.

TAMMIE: You better spill the beans, Rosy Fay Stadtmueller.

ROSY: I heard Greeley was takin' *Spanish* lessons back in July.

TAMMIE: What?

ROSY: Yeah, from Cynthia Morales.

TAMMIE: When?

ROSY: They was seen together at the Oak. He was teachin' *her* how ta *play pool*, and she was teaching him how ta say it all in Mexican.

TAMMIE: Is that all?

ROSY: They say he had his arms all around her. Showin' her how ta *hold the stick*.

TAMMIE: Well, that don't mean—

ROSY: And they say she was drivin' around in his pickup truck.

TAMMIE: His truck!

ROSY: Well, thas' what I heard.

TAMMIE: Nobody drives that truck. He don't even let me drive that truck. Who tole you?

ROSY: I heard it from Rev— *(She stops herself.)* I can't tell you, but it's true. I know it's true.

TAMMIE: Who from?

ROSY: Well…you can't say nothing.

TAMMIE: I ain't .

ROSY: Reverend Pat tole' me. Cuz Cynthia got baptized and born again. She tole' him, so you can't say nothing.

TAMMIE: That Mescun pool hall slut!

ROSY: They'd been drinkin' a course. Maybe even takin' that Spanish Fly.

TAMMIE: She's got big ole tamale eatin' hips!

ROSY: Now hon, watch what stones you throw. She has found Jesus Christ after all.

TAMMIE: Ain't too many men she hadn't found.

ROSY: Tammie! Don't talk that way! Christ is there for anybody who wants Him.

TAMMIE: You know, I got a good mind ta jes' leave him—once and for all. Jes' take that bus on up ta New York City—

ROSY: Oh, now yer talkin' crazy.

TAMMIE: Jes' take a taxi cab right on over ta A B C Studios. I'd wait out there all day long until Tad from *All My Children* comes out—

ROSY: Oh my Lord—

TAMMIE: I'd walk right on up ta him and say: "Excuse me, Tad, I'm Tammie Lynn Schneider from Seguin, Texas, and I jes' traveled two thousand miles on a Greyhound bus ta be yer love slave.

ROSY: Tammie Lynn, you are almost married again. Yer this close. And Greeley's not a bad catch—with a little cleanin' up...and with a little help from Reverend Pat and the Lord. Now's not the time ta be thinkin' about livin' in sin in some Yankee Babylon.

TAMMIE: A lifetime of sin with Tad would be *worth* an eternity of hell fire.

ROSY: Now stop that! You are losin' yer marbles. I'm gonna speak ta Reverend Pat in yer behalf. I have some influence with him. He can talk ta Greeley. He's got a real gift. I bet he could get Greeley ta give up his ways.

TAMMIE: Oh, fat chance.

ROSY: You jes' leave it up ta me. All you gotta do is get Greeley inta church tomorrow.

TAMMIE: Two Sundays in a row? I dragged him kickin' and screamin' last week.

ROSY: This man is in peril! And for that matter, so are you. You gotta devilish look in yer eye.

TAMMIE: I'm gonna get him where it hurts.

ROSY: Where's that?

TAMMIE: I don' know. Put cyanide in his Lone Star.

ROSY: Now that ain't very Christian-like.

TAMMIE: Take a chainsaw to his pickup truck.

ROSY: Maybe revenge ain't the best way, darlin'.

TAMMIE: *(Suddenly hit with an idea)* Oooh, that's jes' too good.

ROSY: What?

TAMMIE: Yeah, that'll get 'im where he lives.

ROSY: Tammie, hon, are you all right?

TAMMIE: I know how I'm gonna get Greeley.

ROSY: You do?

TAMMIE: *("Yep" is like* ED *would say it)* Yep. I'm gonna seduce Ed.

*(Big ole bullfrog, and a quick blackout. End of scene)*

## Scene Three

## The Great Pecan Robbery

*(Setting: Sunday morning.* SHERIFF BART's *office in the Court House Building downtown.)*

*(At rise: Big* SHERIFF BART *(Actor E) is sleeping in his chair. His brand new Deputy,* DIGGITY *[Actor G] comes bursting in.* DIGGITY *sports an awful toupee.)*

DIGGITY: Sheriff. Sheriff Bart! C-C-Come quick. Uh, Uh, uh, you gotta—you gotta—

SHERIFF BART: *(Lurching out of his seat)* Jesus Christ Alive, Diggity, you tryin' ta give me a heart attack?

DIGGITY: But—but—you gotta—you gotta—

SHERIFF BART: Boy, you wanna back out and try knockin' 'fore you come in?

DIGGITY: But you gotta come quick!

SHERIFF BART: I ain't *gotta* do nothing but pay taxes and die.

DIGGITY: We got a robbery on our hands.

SHERIFF BART: Now, now, hole on. Give it to me slow. You say we got some kinda robbery—?

DIGGITY: Outside.

SHERIFF BART: Outside is a mighty big place, boy.

DIGGITY: (As if leading him to the spot) Outside—uh, uh, down the stairs. Uh, uh, down the sidewalk—

SHERIFF BART: You gonna give me dee-rections, Diggity?

DIGGITY: The Great Pecan.

SHERIFF BART: Yeah, I'm there.

DIGGITY: Well, it ain't there.

SHERIFF BART: Say what?

DIGGITY: Somebody went'n took the Great Pecan.

SHERIFF BART: Took the Great—

DIGGITY: There ain't nothing left but the sign.

SHERIFF BART: That thang must weigh a good five hunert pound. It's pure concrete.

DIGGITY: Well, they stole it.

SHERIFF BART: You know who took it, boy?

DIGGITY: No sir. I just saw it gone on my way up here. I don't know how you coulda missed it. It looks naked out there now.

SHERIFF BART: I slep' in the office las' night. Well, whatta we waitin' for? Uh lessee, now I want you ta get out there on the double and get me some infomation on this deal. This is top priority. Don't say nothin' ta nobody yet—especially not ta Mayor Hoppe. He'll have a hissy fit.

DIGGITY: Where do I start?

SHERIFF BART: Well, start asking some of the store owners 'round the square—what time is it now?

DIGGITY: Six-thirty in the A M.

SHERIFF BART: Damn, boy! You crazy? What the hell you doin' here at six-thirty A M?

DIGGITY: I couldn't sleep. First day on the job and all.

SHERIFF BART: Diggity, Diggity, Diggity, you're like a woman at a white sale. *(Beat)* All right. Les' thank this out. That Pecan was there at sevent-thirty las' night cuz I chased a coupla juvenile delinquents off it las' night about that time. That means it happened sometime between yesterday evening and six-thirty this mornin' in the A M. You know who hangs out there late at night is those criminal kids. I want you to go pick up... whas that boy's name—with the ear deal—hangs out with that girl—one whose sister had that operation—cucumber got stuck—took her to the emergency room—doctor had that affair—whas' her name that cuts hair—beauty parlor on Guadalupe—next to the taco place—makes 'em real hot—gives ya flamin' diarrhea for three days—

DIGGITY: Chucky?

SHERIFF BART: Yeah, that's the kid. Pick him up.

DIGGITY: Sheriff Bart. There's—there's one other thang. It was—it was dark out there—

SHERIFF BART: Gonna be dark 'til about seven, Diggity.

DIGGITY: Well, when I was driving up on Court Street, I saw some flashing lights and, and a saucer-like shape—

SHERIFF BART: Diggity, I really don't wanna hear this—

DIGGITY: I gotcha Sheriff, but with that report last Tuesday from Tammie Lynn—

SHERIFF BART: Tammie Lynn Schneider is an A-1 fruitcake, Diggity. Don't you start makin' like squirrel bate on me yer first day on the job.

DIGGITY: Well, I wouldn'ta thought too much of it, but there's these marks on the lawn out there right by the Pecan sign—kinda like circular burn marks—like some kinda circular flame shot down from above— *(He makes sound effect of a spaceship shooting flames.)*

SHERIFF BART: Diggity, I ain't none too cheery at six-thirty in the A M. Takes me a pot of coffee, a breakfast taco, and about three hours 'fore I'm up. Don't be spoutin' off bullcrap ta piss me off 'fore I've had my breakfast taco!

DIGGITY: All I'm sayin' is—

SHERIFF BART: You go wake up Chucky and see what that little som-bitch has ta say fer hisself. Now git.

DIGGITY: This is awful, Sheriff. The Pecan Festival started on Friday. What if we can't find it before the Pecan Parade? They won't be able to crown the Pecan Queen. *(Wistfully)* My dear sweet Mamaw was Pecan Queen back in '47. It's a tradition that goes back a hunerd years.

SHERIFF BART: A hunerd and two, Diggity.

DIGGITY: Lord, this is a disaster.

SHERIFF BART: I'm gonna find that Pecan. Ain't nobody gonna take the Great Pecan out from under my nose and get away with it. Not on my watch. When I find out who did it, I won't jes throw the book, I'll pitch the whole damn library at 'im.

DIGGITY: *(He salutes)* Yes, sir!

SHERIFF BART: Som-bitch.

*(Lights fade to black. End of scene)*

## Scene Four

## Church

*(Setting: Later that Sunday morning. Baptist Church.)*

*(At rise: clunky organ music resounds throughout the church. As the music comes quickly to a climax, ROSY [Actor R] steps shyly out from behind a curtain and takes her seat beside TAMMIE [Actor T]. This is a quick change for Actor G, GREELEY, who comes in late and sits alone on the other side of the church. There is a CONGREGATION of dummy church goers assembled; they could be represented by 2D cut outs, and they are heard on a voice over tape shouting "Amen" occasionally. This is also a quick change for Actor E, REVEREND PAT who soon takes the podium. The REVEREND PAT costume should probably be ready to go under the fat suit of the SHERIFF BART. Please note that when "[uh]" is added to the end of a word, it is meant to punctuate the thought or sentence in a way commonly done by Southern preachers.)*

REVEREND PAT: Thank you, thank you, Miss Rosy for bringing the sweet music of *Jee*-sus inta our lives...for helpin' us bless this very special day, the first Sunday of the Pecan Festival. Come on and let's give her a big "thank ya" folks!

CONGREGATION: *(On a voice-over tape, chants)* Thank you, Rosy.

*(ROSY blushes, and TAMMIE pats her on the back.)*

REVEREND PAT: *(With apparent difficulty—)* Brothers and Sisters...being the confidante of my flock, the ear for the troubled, the eye for the short-sighted...I hear things that happen in this small community. And let me jes' say, before we make our tithe this Sunday, let me jes' address a problem—a Satanic temptation which plagues our society: fornication [uh]! You heard me right! Fornication outta wedlock with a harlot is like fornicatin' with the devil hisself. *(After a beat)* We all, I say, we all, have heard the slippery tongue of the devil calling us—he's out there calling us everyday. But *a few of us* have failed to resist his beck and call, I say *a few of us* have dived headlong into the dark abyss of debauchery. But, people, I say unto you, heed not the devil—no sir—"Let Jesus Christ be the armor that you wear."

CONGREGATION: *(On tape)* Amen, Amen, Pat.

*(*ROSY *and* TAMMIE *stare at* GREELEY *with deep disapproval.)*

ROSY & TAMMIE: *(Joining)* Amen.

*(*GREELEY *seems to be looking to the exit.)*

REVEREND PAT: Folks, Jesus Christ Our Lord knows we are imperfect beings, waging heavily in sin, and that's why He lay down before us the institution of marriage for us to quench these...appetites—sin free! Yes, sir, marriage makes it *legal* in the eyes of the Lord—long as you do it in moderation. But if you ain't married, resist temptation and resist Satan. And if a certain lecherous parta yer anatomy beckons you into the fire, well, let me tell ya what it says in Matthew about that: "If your hand or your foot is your undoing, cut it off and fling it away; it is better for you to enter into life maimed or lame, than to be thrown into the everlasting fires of hell [uh]." *(Beat)* Well, I guess I made ma point. And now, Brothers and Sisters...I'd like to share a conversation I had last night—a conversation I had...with *Jee*-sus. Jesus came to me, he said, "Pat, Pat, I'm coming; I'm coming soon down to the earth with a huge train—I say, a huge train [uh] that seats one million people [uh]. One million souls I'm takin' with me, Pat. And I'll tell ya right now, most of 'um are gonna be Texans!" *(After a beat)* Now I know yer wondering out there, yer palates are salivatin' [uh], yer ears are itchin' [uh], yer askin', "Pat, Pat, how can *I* escape the grim boiling fate of the damned? How can *I* buy a ticket on that ol' SALVATION EXPRESS [uh] first and only stop H-E-A-V-E-N?

CONGREGATION: *(On tape, yells:)* How Pat? How?

REVEREND PAT: *(Quietly)* Well, I'll tell ya. I'll share it with ya. Cuz I love ya. It don't have nothing ta do with how perty ya are. It don't have nothing ta do with how much you know. It don't have nothing ta do with the color a yer skin. Jesus doesn't care if yer black, yer white, yer Mexican, or *Chinese*—long as you have accepted him he does not care. *(Beat) All he cares about* is how much [uh] —how much you give to his works, how much you give to his house, how much you give to *this church* [uh]. It was Matthew who wrote, "Do not store up treasure on earth, where it grows rusty and moth-eaten...store up treasure in heaven!" *(Beat)* Many people come to me, they say, "Pat, Pat, how much shall I give to the church? How much shall I tithe to *Jee*-sus?" Well, I've got a test, a very simple test, I say a child's test, to determine how much you should give. Right now I want you ta look inside yer pocketbook! I want you ta look inside yer checkbook! I want you ta look inside yer *savings account* [uh]! And I want you ta come up with a money figure of what you thank is the absolute most you can give—the absolute most money figure—you—can—give [uh]. *(Beat)* Have ya got a figure? Now I want you ta take that figure, and I want you ta double it—right now—I want you ta double it! Then I want you ta double it again!! And that's how much you should give to the Lord [uh]!! For "it is easier for a camel to pass through the eye of a needle than for a rich man to enter the kingdom of God." The Bible says it—not me. It's His word!

CONGREGATION: Amen.

REVEREND PAT: Now pass them plates!

(GREELEY *feels the eyes of the entire* CONGREGATION, *particularly* ROSY *and* TAMMIE, *as he sifts through the change in his pockets. Lights fade to black. End of scene*)

## Scene 5

## Dueling Seductions

(*Setting: after church. A dual scene: the church office and outside in the church parking lot. Actors freeze when they aren't talking, and lighting brings focus to the active scene.*)

(*At rise:* GREELEY *and* TAMMIE *are having a heated discussion.* ROSY *is filing some papers away in the church office.*)

GREELEY: All right I did it. I came and heard him.

TAMMIE: You heard, but I don't thank you was listenin'.

GREELEY: How could I *not* listen? It's like he set his podium down right in fronta me—the slimy, money grubbin' snake.

TAMMIE: You are goin' straight ta hell, and I ain't going with you.

GREELEY: Look I said I was sorry, *and* I came and sat through a whole sermon without leaving. I don't know what more you want from me.

(TAMMIE *gives* GREELEY *a disgusted look and turns her back on him.* REVEREND PAT *enters the office.*)

ROSY: (*Breathily*) I, I filed those papers on your desk Rev-Revrend Pat.

REVEREND PAT: I could not stop thinkin' about you the whole sermon today!

(REVEREND PAT *begins to maul* ROSY—*kissing her feverishly on the neck and shoulders*)

ROSY: Oh, Rev-Revrend Pat!

TAMMIE: "Sorry's" not a big enough word for what you did.

GREELEY: Look, Tammie, I know I messed thangs up, but I had a little fender bender last week, do not alarm yourself—I am fine, but it cost me seven hunerd dollars just to get a few scratches worked out! Now that in turn threw me completely offa my schedule ta buy you that two thousand dollar engagement ring that you have *insisted* on. Here you are makin' such a big deal ta every Tom, Dick, or Felix that'ud listen—about the ring presentin' fanfare! "Frijole Friday." Be there for the *show*." And due ta circumstances beyond my control, I don't have no ring. So I'm thankin' "I go there Friday night short one ring, Tammie's gonna look foolish". Sweetheart, I just didn't want you ta look foolish in fronta all them people.

TAMMIE: That is the lamest excuse I ever heard. And it jes' goes to prove that that truck's more important to you than I am.

ROSY: Revrend Pat, uh, uh, Revrend Pat. I, uh, Revrend—oh, oh—

(ROSY *runs away from* REVEREND PAT *around the desk.*)

ROSY: Now les' not get carried away.

REVEREND PAT: I can't help but get carried away by you Miss Rosy. It is your intoxicating religious purity which has cast a spell on me. I am as David was for Bathsheba.

ROSY: Bathsheba?

REVEREND PAT: It came to pass in an eveningtide, that I, like David arose from off my bed, and strolled upon the roof of the king's house: and from the roof I saw a woman washing herself; and the woman was very beautiful.

ROSY: What roof would-would this be?

(REVEREND PAT *continues to maul* ROSY.)

GREELEY: I was backed into a corner. What was I supposed ta do? I ain't made of money! I thought you was marrying me for me. Greeley. I am Greeley, and I ain't no other.

TAMMIE: Well, if you was backed into a corner, you have tuh back into a corner over't the Seven Eleven?

GREELEY: It is a sad day in Texas when idle gossip mongers ruin a promising future of rosy, marital bliss.

ROSY: I'm not sure if this is right, Revrend Pat. You're wife...

REVEREND PAT: *(With utmost sincerity)* Rosy, Rosy, you have stoked the fire of my religious fervor. I am a man who is ensnared in a trap. When I see you before my glorious organ, magically stroking those keys, shooting ethereal melodies through those rigid pipes, I feel as if I could reach out and touch the cloak of God. Yet it says in the book of James, "Let no man say when he is tempted, 'I am tempted by God': for God cannot tempt any one." I am in agony.

ROSY: Agony?

REVEREND PAT: Agony. "Can a man take fire in his bosom, and his clothes not be burned?" Ah, too late. Too late.

ROSY: But it's not too late...we haven't done anything, Revrend Pat.

REVEREND PAT: Oh, my sweet, sweet girl, "whoever looketh on a woman to lust after her hath committed adultery with her already in his heart".

(ROSY *ponders this one for a moment.*)

TAMMIE: Okay, Greeley, I am a Christian, and as such I can forgive.

GREELEY: Oh, thank you, Tammie. You are the pecan in my pie.

TAMMIE: But just because I forgive, don't mean I forget.

ROSY: So even without even doing anything—

REVEREND PAT: —we are already steeped in sin.

TAMMIE: And there will be a task for you—a penance.

GREELEY: A—a—say what?

TAMMIE: Somethin' you gotta do ta prove ta me where your loyalties lie.

ROSY: I think of you too, Revrend Pat.

REVEREND PAT: Poor, sweet dear.

ROSY: I thought they were just thoughts—

REVEREND PAT: —if only they were.

GREELEY: What're we talkin' about here?

TAMMIE: You gotta give me your truck this weekend.

GREELEY: My truck! Why would I give you my truck?

TAMMIE: Cuz' I wanna drive it in the Pecan Parade.

ROSY: The thoughts are already sins. What can we do?

REVEREND PAT: Luckily we are blessed.

ROSY: We are?

(REVEREND PAT *crosses to get his bible.*)

GREELEY: Tammie, Tammie, you know the Greeley truck creed: "Nobody but the Greeley drives the truck."

TAMMIE: Nobody?

GREELEY: I'm surprised at you, Tammie. You know my truck creed.

TAMMIE: I know, but I thought maybe there might be special extenuatin' circumstances when you might break your truck creed. Like maybe you might like some girl so much you say, "To hell with the creed, I just wanna get laid."

(GREELEY *looks shocked.*)

REVEREND PAT: We are blessed, Miss Rosy. We who are "the children of disobedience indulging the desires of the flesh...but God, who is rich in mercy, even when we were dead in our sins, hath quickened us together with Christ."

ROSY: Praise the Lord.

(REVEREND PAT *and* ROSY *start making out.*)

GREELEY: Tammie, we have never had sex in the whole two years we've known each other even though I have begged you repeatedly.

TAMMIE: I'm just speaking like a hypothetical.

GREELEY: Are we talkin' about foolin' around?

REVEREND PAT: How about a swim in the baptistry, Miss Rosy?

ROSY: Are you sure?

REVEREND PAT: We have already sinned in our hearts, Miss Rosy. We might as well enjoy it.

(REVEREND PAT *and* ROSY *exit into the baptistry, losing a few garments as they go.*)

TAMMIE: Would you ever let someone else drive it in exchange for sex?

GREELEY: Well, you lost me. I thought I was with ya, but—

TAMMIE: Like say, Cynthia Morales.

GREELEY: Cynthia Morales. I don't believe I know any Cynthia Morales.

TAMMIE: That's not what I heard.

GREELEY: Who's she sposed to be?

TAMMIE: Some slut who drove your truck, I heard.

GREELEY: Drove my—! Now somebody's been tellin' you tall tales, honey pie. You know my truck creed. Thas just horse pooky.

TAMMIE: You had better be tellin' me the truth, Greeley.

GREELEY: Tammie, *puh*-lease.

TAMMIE: You think yer the only fish in the sea? You think yer the only man interested in me?

GREELEY: *(After a brief thought)* Yeah.

TAMMIE: Well, that just ain't true. There are plenty of men interested in me.

GREELEY: Like who?

TAMMIE: Ed.

(GREELEY *can't help but chuckle at the improbable match.)*

TAMMIE: Thas right…laugh. Jes' laugh. You'll see.

*(Lights fade to black. End of scene)*

## Scene 6

### The Future Pecan Queen

*(Setting: Sunday, early afternoon. The bathroom of* PRISCILLA ROTTWEILER.)

*(At rise: This is a relatively quick change for Actor R.* PRISCILLA *[Actor R] is looking at herself in the mirror.)*

PRISCILLA: *(Presenting a delicate, thoughtful address)* Thank you. Thank you, one and all. I'd like to thank

the members of the selection committee for this
great honor. I am sure it could not have been an easy
decision considering all of the intelligent, beautiful
contenders for the crown— *(As she nods to each of the
losers)* —Tawnya Blackhorn, DeAndra Loogan, Cynthia
Morales. Wonderful, wonderful competitors all. I
pledge that I will wear the crown of Pecan Queen with
pride and distinction for the year to come. No thank
you speech would be complete without thanking my
dear, dear family—my baby brother, Deke, my father,
head engineer of Structural Metals, Inc— *(Waving
to Daddy)* —hi, Daddy. And lastly, but certainly not
leastly, my mother, who, by example, has taught me
the true meaning of womanhood—

*(PRISCILLA's mother, MRS ROTTWEILER [Actor T] knocks
on the bathroom door. Her voice is muffled.)*

MRS ROTTWEILER: *(O S)* Priscilla? Priscilla dear—

PRISCILLA: *(Her beauty queen demeanor becoming
absolutely Satanic)* WHAAAAAAAT! I'm practicing my
speech for Christsake!

MRS ROTTWEILER: *(O S)* Supper's ready, honey.

PRISCILLA: Oh, for the love of God, Mother, just start
without me!

MRS ROTTWEILER: *(O S)* I fixed that low fat meatloaf just
like you wanted.

PRISCILLA: I'm in the middle of my speech! I'll be down
in a minute! *Comprende inglese?*

MRS ROTTWEILER: Okie dokie, honey.

*(PRISCILLA lets loose an exaggerated sigh as she tries to
recompose that sweet, dutiful demeanor.)*

PRISCILLA: Hi, Daddy. Hi, Daddy.

(PRISCILLA *can't quite remember what comes next, so she takes a deep breath until it comes to her. In the following section she mispronounces "Camus".)*

PRISCILLA: Hi, Daddy. And lastly, but certainly not leastly, my mother, who by example has taught me the true meaning of womanhood. *Je t'aime, ma mere.* I think it was that wise philosopher, Camus, who said, "This is the dog's dick." *(Beat)* Oh, my. Did I just say, "dick"? Mercy me. I have just said "dick" and turned you all into horny toads. Dick, dick, dick. Dog's dick. *(Like she is doing a newsflash)* "Pecan Queen shocks the world— says `dick' in front of an adoring crowd of onlookers." Now that I'm Pecan Queen, there are going to be a few changes around here. First of all, DeAndra Loogan, you will carry my train for the entire year—always following a respectful twenty-eight steps behind. I have a veeery long train.

(PRISCILLA*'s little brother,* DEKE *[Actor G] knocks at the door)*

PRISCILLA: *WHAAAAAT?*

DEKE: *(O S)* I gotta pee.

PRISCILLA: So go in a bottle, that's why you got that little wiener.

DEKE: *(O S)* It's supper anyway.

PRISCILLA: Leave me alone, you little retard. I'm practicing my speech.

DEKE: *(O S)* I gotta go.

PRISCILLA: Go—down—*STAIRS!!* Why do you think we have three bathrooms?

DEKE: *(O S)* Priss.

PRISCILLA: Geek! *(Beat)* Oh, oh, my dear fans! To subject you to such ugliness is such an unthinkable breech of etiquette. Where was I? This will be the year when the Pecan Queen makes a difference. This will be the year when the Pecan Queen takes some action—solves World Hunger. World Peace. And combats gaucherie in all its forms. This I promise.

(PRISCILLA *waves and nods to the masses in the mirror. Lights fade to black. End of scene)*

## Scene 7

## The Interrogation

*(Setting: Sunday Afternoon. Sheriff's Office.)*

*(At rise:* SHERIFF BART *[Actor E] is doing some paperwork.* DIGGITY *[Actor G] comes bursting into the room with* CHUCKY CONNORS *[Actor T] in handcuffs.* SHERIFF BART *is so startled he just about goes through the roof. Papers fly everywhere.)*

DIGGITY: I GOT THE LIL' SOM-BITCH!

CHUCKY: Let me go you fascist pig!

DIGGITY: What'd you call me, you little fruit?

SHERIFF BART: Jesus Christ Alive, Diggity, you're gonna give me a stroke 'fore this day is done.

DIGGITY: S-S-Sorry, Sheriff.

SHERIFF BART: Knock, Diggity. Knock! You gotta knock 'fore you come in.

DIGGITY: D-Did you want me ta come back in?

SHERIFF BART: What the hell for? Yer in now.

DIGGITY: Well, I got him.

SHERIFF BART: I can see that. Did he give you much trouble?

DIGGITY: Not much. I just clocked him in the shin with my night stick, then put the choke hold on him, and he was begging me to cuff him.

SHERIFF BART: Diggity, I realize it's yer first day, and you wanna do good, but you can't go 'round choke holdin' the citizens of Seguin—not even little fruits like this earring wearing piece-a soiled t.p. Now uncuff him.

DIGGITY: You sure, Sheriff?

SHERIFF BART: Yeah, I'm sure. I'm the Sheriff, ain't I?

DIGGITY: Yes, you are, Sheriff Bart! I found this on him too, sir!

(DIGGITY *produces a Lone Star beer bottle. Pause as* SHERIFF BART *takes in* CHUCKY CONNORS)

SHERIFF BART: Now what would yer mamma say if she knew you was drinkin' beer, Chucky?

CHUCKY: She'd probably say, "Save one for me, you little terd."

DIGGITY: You answer the Sheriff nice, boy, or I might rip that earring right off.

SHERIFF BART: Chucky, Chucky, Chucky, what am I gonna do with you?

DIGGITY: Keep him in the holdin' cell for a few days with the real criminals.

CHUCKY: (*Sarcastically*) Yeah, right. All those rapists and murderers you got in there.

SHERIFF BART: You know, Diggity, this boy is right. Only guy in there now is Langley, and he's in there for bein' a drunk. No, about the worst criminal we got in town right now is Chucky.

CHUCKY: I ain't no criminal.

SHERIFF BART: You already spent six months in Juvey Hall last year for masterminding that Bull Semen heist in Marion.

DIGGITY: Sick little freak.

SHERIFF BART: Now where did you think you was gonna fence four thousand dollars worth of bull semen?

CHUCKY: I didn't do it for the money.

DIGGITY: Maybe he likes to drink it.

SHERIFF BART: Diggity, I just had my lunch.

DIGGITY: Sorry, Sheriff.

CHUCKY: I did it for the oppressed bull.

DIGGITY: This kid don't even think like a Texan.

SHERIFF BART: His family just moved here from up north.

DIGGITY: A Yankee. I thought he smelled funny.

SHERIFF BART: All right, boy, so tell me what you got against the Great Pecan. You trying to free all the oppressed nuts?

CHUCKY: I don't know what you're talking about.

DIGGITY: Don't chew get cute now, boy.

SHERIFF BART: We got reason to believe you stole the Great Pecan.

CHUCKY: The giant nut statue? Somebody stole it?

SHERIFF BART: Yeah, *somebody* did.

DIGGITY: You did.

CHUCKY: Now why would I wanna steal that big joke?

DIGGITY: Don't talk about the Pecan that way, Yankee.

CHUCKY: What is it with that thing? Some guy tried to tell me it was real when I first got here.

DIGGITY: It is real.

CHUCKY: Yeah, and so is your hair.

DIGGITY: Shut up!

SHERIFF BART: So yer tellin' me you didn't have nothin' ta do with it?

CHUCKY: No, but now that I think about it, it's a pretty good idea. Have everybody cryin' about a big old piece of concrete. I wish I had thought of it.

DIGGITY: Sheriff, you gotta let me have just five minutes alone with him.

SHERIFF BART: Diggity. *(Beat)* Now how can I believe a little chicken shit delinquent like you? Where were you last night?

CHUCKY: I was cruising the Sonic drive thru like every other red blooded Seguinite, whatta you think?

SHERIFF BART: Were you with anybody?

CHUCKY: I was trying to be with somebody, but it didn't work out.

DIGGITY: You better start givin' some straight answers.

CHUCKY: That's the truth. I was by myself, but plenty of people saw me.

SHERIFF BART: How late was you out?

CHUCKY: 'Til three.

DIGGITY: I'm tellin' you Sheriff, this town needs a curfew.

CHUCKY: Can I go now?

DIGGITY: You go when the Sheriff says you can go.

SHERIFF BART: Let him go.

DIGGITY: *Now* you can go.

SHERIFF BART: But remember, the eyes of Texas are upon you. You're still a prime suspect in this incident.

CHUCKY: Yeah, well, it's been nice chattin' with you. *(He exits.)*

DIGGITY: I think we shoulda held him.

SHERIFF BART: He'll mess up, Diggity, and when he does we'll be waitin'.

DIGGITY: Sheriff, is my hair on crooked?

SHERIFF BART: You know who hangs out around town at all hours of the night and mighta seen something is that guy—has that funny hair—momma's in the state home—her som-bitch brother has that feed store over on Austin Street—next to the theatre—say his wife sleeps around—sposed ta have that tattoo on her butt of a winking Jesus—kinda like the one that drunk ole coot, Dexter, has on his bicep—what's that boy's name—you know the homo—?

DIGGITY: Francio?

SHERIFF BART: Yeah, Francio. Let's track him down—see if he happened ta be hangin' around during the heist.

DIGGITY: Where do we keep the rubber gloves?

SHERIFF BART: I don't want you to rough him up, Diggity, I just want to ask him a few questions.

*(The phone rings, and* DIGGITY *jumps to pick it up, but a sharp look from* SHERIFF BART *holds him at bay.)*

SHERIFF BART: Sheriff here. *(Beat)* Say what? How'd you find that out? *(Beat)* Yeah, I'll make a statement. All I got to say is that all the resources of the Sheriff's department are focused on the case. The Great Pecan will be found before the Pecan Parade. *(He hangs up the phone.)* The pooch is screwed.

DIGGITY: The press?

SHERIFF BART: Worse. My wife.

*(The lights snap to black. End of scene)*

## SCENE 8

### Pecan Serenade

*(Setting: Sunday evening. ED's porch.)*

*(At rise: This is a quick change for Actor E who will enter as ED. The radio plays in the dark for a bit. Speaking on tape will be JOHNNY JOHNS [Actor G] and BILLY POMGRANITE [Actor E], a pecan expert.)*

JOHNNY JOHNS: *(V O)* This is Johnny Johns at KWAD. Folks, it's pecan season out there, and we have Billy Pomgranite here to talk to us about what to look for, the best time to harvest, and all that good stuff. Hey, Billy.

BILLY POMGRANITE: Hey Johnny. Thanks for havin' me on.

JOHNNY JOHNS: Well, this season the pecans are as plentiful as the toilet paper falsies in a beauty contest.

BILLY POMGRANITE: They are, they are, Johnny. It's a good harvest.

JOHNNY JOHNS: Now if a pecan falls offa tree, and there's nobody there to hear it, does it make a noise?

BILLY POMGRANITE: Johnny not only does it make a thud, but it literally screams out to the world, "Somebody eat me!"

*(The lights rise on ED sitting on a picnic table. He turns off the radio. He's got a bucket of unshelled pecans on one side of him and a ceramic bowl of shelled nuts on the other side. He methodically works at shelling a pecan.)*

ED: This is a rare nut. *(He takes the shelled jewel with theindex finger and thumb of both hands and carefully offers it up to his nose for an extended whiff—just the right nostril. Then he shakes his head jerkily like he is clearing his palette and let's out an enormous sigh that is almost like passing gas.)* A rare nut indeed. Perfect bouquet. Ripened to perfection. Spawned from a mature tree, a buxom fifty year old beauty. What a precious jewel. The Texas Pecan. *(Beat)* This one here is a *Desirable*. Pure gold. Now your *Shawnee's* not a bad piece of meat, no, no, no...some people prefer the delicate size and texture of a *Schley*...but the *Desirable* is the Dom Perignon of Pecans. This particular nut is the most *desirable* I've seen this year. Self control...self control. It'll bring a pretty price. Got to remember that. No, no, this one's not for eating. *(He produces a small golden box from out of nowhere which pops open rather mysteriously. He carefully lays the pecan inside, presses a button on the box, and it snaps shut. As he dances around the box, slowly stripping off his clothes, he begins to sing—)*

Remember, amigo.
The pecan is fleetin'.
So don't be cheatin'.
Like some dumb cretin.
This nut is not for eatin'!
Oh, yippee, yai-yaaaay. Yippee, yai-youuuu.
Say, yippee, yai-yaaaay. Yippee, yai-youuuu.

*(ED's last bits of yodeling turn into some otherwordly screech. The lights snap to black. Note: For the* Pecan Serenade *you may make up your own tune, or alternatively music by David Marantz is available for licensing. End of scene)*

## Scene 9

## Beauty Day

*(Setting: Sonja's Beauty Parlor. Monday morning)*

*(At rise:* SONJA GUAREZ *[Actor R], the owner of a beauty parlor named, "SONJA'S," is cleaning her scissors and opening up shop as she listens to a radio program on KWAD [on tape]).*

JOHNNY JOHNS: *(V O)* Hey there folks, this is Johnny Johns reminding you that you can get yer Pecan Festival makeover at Sonja's Beauty Parlor here in town. Sonja's been a judge and wonderful supporter of the Pecan Queen Pageant for about ten years now, and she knows beauty like the back of her hand. That's Sonja's on Guadalupe. *(Short beat)* We're gonna kill a little time here at KWAD…play a few songs…here's your favorite and mine…

*(*TAMMIE *[Actor T] makes a hurried entrance.* SONJA *turns the radio off)*

TAMMIE: Sorry I'm late.

SONJA: Am I surprised?

TAMMIE: Mrs Bart isn't here yet is she?

SONJA: No, she's late too. Fortune shines on you today.

TAMMIE: I had just the most horrible night last night. I could not sleep a wink.

SONJA: Lemme guess, Greeley blew the ring money.

TAMMIE: No.

SONJA: Greeley, had an affair.

TAMMIE: No.

SONJA: *Ay, dios mio,* Greeley totaled the truck.

TAMMIE: No worse.

SONJA: What could be worse?

TAMMIE: *(Secretively)* Ed is an alien.

SONJA: Tammie, I know *Mexicanos*, and he ain't no wetback.

TAMMIE: I don't mean and illegal alien. I mean a space alien.

SONJA: *Ay, pobrecita*, space aliens again. Didn't I tell you where drinking would lead you? Off your marbles like my ex-husband, Frank.

TAMMIE: I am not drunk, I have not been drunk, I do not drink. Ed is an alien!

*(FRANCIO [Actor G] an effeminate misfit with a heart of gold, comes in the door)*

SONJA: What chew want, baby?

FRANCIO: I need a manicure, baby. I gonna enter the Pecan Queen Contest.

SONJA: I will give you a manicure, baby, but I won't put no more red polish on. It's clear polish or nothing.

FRANCIO: Red's my color, baby.

SONJA: Black and blue's gonna be your color, *baby*. Clear or not at all.

FRANCIO: Okay clear.

SONJA: Now you got it, baby. *(Indicating a chair)* Hop up here. *(Beat, sincerely)* Now promise me, baby. Don't go down to the Pageant again in drag. Last time you did that, what happened? You got in big trouble.

FRANCIO: But iss not fair, baby.

SONJA: I know, I know. *Mira*...you are my Beauty Queen, okay baby?

FRANCIO: Okay.

SONJA: All right then. *(Short beat)* Hey, Francio, Tammie thinks her neighbor's a space monster.

TAMMIE: Sonja!

SONJA: Oh, it's all right. Francio don't care. Right, baby?

FRANCIO: You got it, baby.

SONJA: Oh my god, I wish I had hands like these. You have got the hands of a model, and I am not lying. *Muy lindos.*

FRANCIO: *Es verdad*, baby.

SONJA: Tammie, look at these beautiful hands.

TAMMIE: I've seen 'em.

SONJA: You shave the hair offa yer knuckles?

FRANCIO: Pluck it—one by one.

SONJA: *Ay, yai, yai.* The price of beauty. *(Beat)* So tell me the story, Tammie. Why is Ed an alien?

TAMMIE: Well, I decided to get a little revenge on Greeley for cheating on me—

SONJA: —with Jewel Bauerbom.

TAMMIE: Say what? I didn't say nothin' about Jewel Bauerbom.

SONJA: Oh, never mind.

TAMMIE: Did you hear something about Greeley and her?

SONJA: No, no, no.

FRANCIO: I heard something, baby.

TAMMIE: What'd you hear?

FRANCIO: She was gassing up his truck.

TAMMIE: She was…she was gassing—do you mean she was driving it?

FRANCIO: I guess she was driving it if she was gassing it. That's just what I heard.

TAMMIE: Who told you that?

FRANCIO: I can't reveal my sources, baby. Thas' top secret.

TAMMIE: WHO TOLD YOU THAT?!

FRANCIO: Owww!

SONJA: Tammie, I almost ripped through his cuticle.

TAMMIE: I'm sorry.

FRANCIO: Wendy at the Seven Eleven tol' me. She was pissed at Greeley cuz he don't let her drive no more.

TAMMIE: He don't let her drive what?

FRANCIO: The truck.

TAMMIE: Greeley's truck?!

FRANCIO: Thas' what I said.

TAMMIE: *(Getting panicky)* Wendy drove…*nobody* drives Greeley's truck. He's—he's got the creed, the Greeley truck creed: "Nobody but the Greeley drives the truck." Nobody drives it.

FRANCIO: Thas' what I heard. Thas' all.

SONJA: Tammie, you better calm down. You got Mrs. Sheriff's wife coming in here any minute for a perm.

TAMMIE: But I don't understand. Ed's an alien. Every woman in Seguin drives Greeley's truck. None of it makes sense.

SONJA: I never drived it.

FRANCIO: Me neither, baby.

SONJA: So tell us about Ed, Tammie, before you pass out.

TAMMIE: I went over there to seduce Ed.

FRANCIO & SONJA: Ed! Eeewww!

TAMMIE: That's Greeley's best friend these days. I thought it would make him think twice about foolin' around on me anymore.

SONJA: *(Sarcastically)* Oh, this is a good plan.

TAMMIE: Well, I got there, and there was this glow around the back of the house—you know he lives out in the country—nobody around for miles. Well, I go around the side, and I see Ed completely naked—

SONJA: Eeeewww!

FRANCIO: Without nothing?

TAMMIE: —naked as the day he was born, dancin' and hoppin' 'round what looked like—what appeared to be—the Great Pecan.

SONJA: What? The Great Pecan—?

FRANCIO: —in his back yard?

TAMMIE: Or some facsimile. So he's dancin' around there, howlin' like a banshee, naked as a jaybird, and I'm thinkin' well this ain't *so* weird. But then all of a sudden, his ears started ta glow and steam started ta shoot outta his armpits.

FRANCIO: B O, baby.

TAMMIE: I'm not makin' this up!

SONJA: We know yer not, honey. Calm down. I'm sure there's some kind of explanation.

TAMMIE: Yes, yes, an explanation—very clear—Ed is from outer space.

(MRS BART, SHERIFF BART's *wife [Actor E] sashays in the door)*

MRS BART: My, my, my, my, my. What a day. What a day.

TAMMIE: Not a word now.

SONJA: We thought you were abducted by space aliens, Mrs. Bart.

MRS BART: Happily, that is not true, though if it were, I am quite sure the space aliens would congratulate themselves on acquiring such a stunning example of wit, wisdom, and personal style. How are you girls today—oh!

(MRS BART *notices* FRANCIO *and clearly does not approve, though she attempts civility.*)

MRS BART: I did not realize you had *other* customers here.

SONJA: Well, Mrs Bart, we try to get as many in here as we can.

MRS BART: Yes, well, hello.

FRANCIO: Hello, baby.

MRS BART: Yes, well, I am here for my—

TAMMIE: —perm—

MRS BART: —perm, Tammie, and you can take a look at the roots. I may need a dye job too, if you're not too terribly busy. My husband, the, uh—

SONJA: —the sheriff—

MRS BART: —the sheriff likes me to look like a young thang, and I do my best to please my man.

FRANCIO: Now yer talkin' baby.

MRS BART: Yes, yes. Well, where shall I—

TAMMIE: Sit over here, Mrs Bart.

MRS BART: All right, Tammie. Make me beautiful! (*Laughing*) I don't mind taking a load off my feet. Oh, girls, girls, and—

(MRS BART *looks at* FRANCIO *and decides it's best not to categorize.*)

MRS BART: —have you heard the latest? Have you heard? I've been telling everybody in town: the Great Pecan has been stolen!

(FRANCIO *shrieks.* SONJA *and* TAMMIE *look to each other—* SONJA *in shock,* TAMMIE *justified—as the lights snap to black.*)

END OF ACT ONE

# ACT TWO

## Scene 1

### Greeley's Creed

*(Setting:* ED's *porch. Thursday night)*

*(At rise:* ED, GREELEY, *and the crickets)*

GREELEY: Ed?

ED: Yeah, Greeley.

GREELEY: That a shootin' star?

ED: Yep.

*(Crickets chirp.)*

GREELEY: Damn that's bright.

ED: Yep.

GREELEY: Yep. Ed? I am a failure as a man. Every man's gotta have a creed. You've got *your* creed. I've got mine.

ED: Yep.

GREELEY: My creed is a farce, Ed.

ED: Sorry to hear it.

GREELEY: What's the Greeley creed?

ED & GREELEY: *(Together)* "Only the Greeley drives the truck."

ED: Good creed.

GREELEY: Damn straight it's a good creed. It defines the relationship between a Texan and his most valued possession—his truck. A truck is like a temple. A thing of impressive physical beauty...glossy, sleek metal structure...sparklin' silver chromed trim... his sanctuary...rugged, thick treaded, black rubber wheels...that mystic circle which takes him on his journey...gun rack, an altar where a man lays his source of power and magic, his deadly boom stick, provider of food and sport. Ed, a man's truck is his mobile Fortress of Solitude. Driving late at night on an old country road, the steady hum of rollin' rubber drawing you forward over an asphalt galaxy, listenin' ta the wistful wails of Waylon Jennings, an infinite universe swirlin' above in the inky firmament. It's more sacred than any baptism, any confirmation, any last rites. *(Beat)* I've broken my truck creed, Ed.

ED: Spill it, brother.

GREELEY: I have let five women drive my truck, Ed, and not one of them has been my fiancee: Cynthia Morales, Wendy Sparks, Jewel Bauerbom, DeAndra Loogan, and June Rottweiler. All in hopes of gettin' laid, and I have yet to get any.

ED: That is so sad.

GREELEY: And even worse punishment, Jewel Bauerbom ran right into the pump guard at Seven Eleven and put a horrible dent in my driver's side door. It cost me seven hunerd dollars to return it to the mint condition befitting such a holy shrine.

*(ED belches.)*

GREELEY: So I promised myself, Ed, I vowed before the heavens, I would no longer trade in my creed for carnal satisfaction. From this point forth no woman, nay, nor man neither will drive the sacred transport.

ED: Uh, oh.

GREELEY: Tammie wants it this Saturday…ta drive in
the Pecan Parade. She's been hearing rumors about the
other women, and she wants to stake her claim. Not
only that, but Tammie says Revrend Pat says Jesus says
he's pissed off at me, and I need 'bout five Sundays
in a row to make up for it. I don't think I can take that
torture, but I don't wanna go to hell or anythang.

ED: Yep.

GREELEY: I love Tammie, I do, Ed, but I'm scared. She's
trying ta turn me inta somethin' that I ain't. Some
kinda holy-roller choir boy. Dudn't she see it's useless?
Eventually the mold will shatter, and there will stand
Greeley—no metamorphized butterfly, no beautiful
thing—only Greeley.

(Crickets)

ED: On my planet, we believe in God. We believe in the
same God that most of your Bible refers to—a loving,
forgiving creator, who has formed us in his image.
But to your God you have added a dimension whose
origin we cannot fathom: egomania. You believe that
God needs you to adore Him. Counts the number
of times you appear in a worship house. Tallies the
times you evoke Him in prayer. That He shines his
favor on only *one* religion. (Short beat) Prayer is for
you, my friend, not God. You worship Him in deeds,
not by attendance records. The most holy act is to
bestow love and selflessness on one of His creatures.
To share your truck with one woman—*one woman*—is
not the transgression of a creed, but the beginning of
a transfiguration—a new creed. The woman to share
your truck with is right in front of you, my friend. In
time, you'll see her.

(Crickets)

GREELEY: Ed...did you just say, "on my planet"?

*(Lights fade to black. End of scene)*

## Scene 2

## The Future Queen Slips Into Despair

*(Setting: The bathroom of* PRISCILLA. *Friday morning)*

*(At rise:* PRISCILLA *[Actor R] wears her Pecan Queen evening gown—though it looks as though it's been slept in several nights. Her hair is a mess.* MRS ROTTWEILER *[Actor T] knocks lightly on the door and comes into the bathroom with oven mitts on her hands.)*

MRS ROTTWEILER: Priscilla! Priscilla, honey, come eat some breakfast.

PRISCILLA: I don't want anythang.

MRS ROTTWEILER: Priscilla, baby, it's been three days now. You have got to put some food into that body of yours.

PRISCILLA: I'm on a hunger strike, Mother.

MRS ROTTWEILER: Priscilla, what in the world kinda good will that do? When you don't eat the only person it affects is you.

PRISCILLA: What are you making?

MRS ROTTWEILER: Chocolate chip pancakes, your favorite.

PRISCILLA: Too fattening.

MRS ROTTWEILER: You haven't eaten in three days, dear, I think you can afford a little fat.

PRISCILLA: *(Beginning to weep)* My life is over.

MRS ROTTWEILER: Priscilla, you have every opportunity
in the world. Opportunities I never had—gettin'
married to your dad so young.

PRISCILLA: Why did they have to steal the Pecan? Why?
What kind of...*sicko* would do that?

MRS ROTTWEILER: Well, it takes all kinds to make a
world.

PRISCILLA: Well, I could do very well without that kind,
thank you. Some demented deviant who preys on the
hopes of young girls. Who dashes the dewy dreams
of a community by his actions. Without the Pecan
Festival, where will we all be?

MRS ROTTWEILER: Oh, I imagine life will go on pretty
much as before.

PRISCILLA: You don't see it, Mother. You don't have
the vision. This is not just—just some big party—
WAHOOO. *(With holy reverence)* The Great Pecan is the
very identity, the very *soul* of our community. Think
of all those young girls in elementary and junior high
school, watching in awe the crowning of the city's
favorite daughter, The Pecan Queen. "Someday that
will be me," they say, "Someday, I too will make my
mark in history." What will we Seguinites do without
our symbol of fertility and renewal—without the
Great, Great Pecan?

*(Beat, the light changes, and* PRISCILLA *enters a dream trial
where she is the prosecutor.)*

PRISCILLA: Ladies and Gentlemen of the jury. There
he sits. There sits the fiend who soiled our innocence,
who raped the Great Pecan. He has no remorse for
what he's done. When you bring back a verdict, the
only verdict you *can* bring back, we ask that you
recommend the strictest punishment the law allows for
this heinous crime...*the death penalty!*

MRS ROTTWEILER: Honey, you really oughtta eat something. You're rambling now.

(MRS ROTTWEILER *exits into* PRISCILLA*'s bedroom for a moment and comes back with a furry pink phone with a very, very long cord.*)

PRISCILLA: Silence in the court! I'll have you in shackles.

MRS ROTTWEILER: I'm calling Doctor Loogan.

PRISCILLA: Quack, quack, quack, quack, quack.

(MRS ROTTWEILER *dials the phone.*)

MRS ROTTWEILER: Hello, I'd like to make an appointment to see Doctor Loogan. Yes, I'll hold.

PRISCILLA: I'd like to thank the members of the selection committee for this great honor. I am sure it could not have been an easy decision considering all of the intelligent, beautiful contenders for the crown— Tawnya "Unibrow" Blackhorn, DeAndra "Nose Job" Loogan, Cynthia "Fat Ass" Morales. (*Continuing her speech under the next few lines of* MRS ROTTWEILER—) No thank you speech would be complete without thanking my dear, dear family—my baby brother, Deke, my father, head engineer of Structural Metals— hi, Daddy…hi, Daddy…hi, Daddy….

MRS ROTTWEILER: Well, I think my daughter is having a nervous breakdown or something. Do you think he could work me in? (*Beat*) Thank you. We'll see you in an hour.

(PRISCILLA *continues as much of her speech as she has time for before the lights slowly fade to black. End of scene*)

## Scene 3

## Tammie On The Verge Of A Nervous Breakdown

*(Setting: The Church Office. Friday afternoon)*

*(At rise:* REVEREND PAT *[Actor E] is having a consultation with* TAMMIE *[Actor T]. This is a quick change for Actor T.)*

TAMMIE: *(Speaking with rapid fire manic speed)* So Ed's an alien, and he kidnapped the Great Pecan. And I'm thinking maybe we should do something, like put him in a test tube or dissect him or something. And Greeley...Greeley's letting every woman in Seguin drive his truck except me. And I'm not getting married obviously because Greeley is a huge liar. He's supposed to let me drive his truck for the parade tomorrow, but I can't get him on the phone. He disappeared. And the Pecan's part of some alien experiment, so the parade will probably be called off. And Greeley will use that as an excuse to call off the engagement. And I'm past the age where anyone else will marry me, including aliens, because Greeley's kept me strung along for so long.

REVEREND PAT: Hmmmm. I see. *(Beat)* Let me ask you, my dear, are you on any medication?

TAMMIE: No, I am not!

REVEREND PAT: Have you seen a doctor?

TAMMIE: Revrend Pat, I thought that you...I am not making this up. Now, I came to you for help—

*(*ROSY *[Actor R] comes in.)*

ROSY: Revrend Pat, I need to talk—

REVEREND PAT: Rosy, dear, I'm talking to one of my flock right now. Can you give me a few minutes?

ROSY: Well, this is important.

TAMMIE: Yeah, Rosy, like my whole damn life exploding ain't important.

REVEREND PAT: Rosy, please—

ROSY: All right. (*She leaves.*)

TAMMIE: I am searching for answers, Revrend. And I thought you—

REVEREND PAT: Tammie, I know this—this—Ed, is getting under your skin. And you wonder what ought to be done. But let me ask you this. Can't you just let him be? You know, there is a quote from the Bible— from Leviticus— "The alien living with you must be treated as one of your native-born. Love him as yourself, for you were aliens in Egypt." Now I believe the sentiment was not originally meant to encompass extraterrestrial beings—

TAMMIE: You don't believe me, do you?

REVEREND PAT: I believe that you believe. And that is what's important.

TAMMIE: You've said in sermons that ghosts and goblins and U F Os were all tricks of the devil. Something has to be done!

REVEREND PAT: Tammie, *if* Ed is an alien, then it's up to Jesus to do whatever the something is that has to be done. Or it's up to the church. Or the lawful authorities. I don't think it's up to you.

TAMMIE: Double talk. Double talk. All this double talk and meanwhile, Greeley is fornicating with every woman in Seguin.

REVEREND PAT: The one has nothing to do with the other, as far as I can tell. Let's be rational—

TAMMIE: (*Getting up*) Rational! Rational! How can anyone be rational in this situation? You were my last

hope, Revrend. My last hope. But words are no good
any more. Now it's time for action.

REVEREND PAT: Tammie Lynn, please sit back down!

(TAMMIE *sits.*)

REVEREND PAT: Now as far as Greeley is concerned,
he just needs to be shown the light. He needs some
powerful persuasion, but it has been done, and it can
be done—

(*A lighting bolt of an idea hits* TAMMIE *in the head.*)

TAMMIE: Persuasion! Yes, of course, *powerful*
persuasion…it's clear now. It's all so clear.

REVEREND PAT: Now Tammie, let's—

TAMMIE: Thank you, Revrend, you've been a big help.

REVEREND PAT: Tammie—

(ROSY *bursts in.*)

ROSY: Are you finished now?

REVEREND PAT: Well, actually—

TAMMIE: Yes, Rosy, we are finished. Thank you,
Revrend Pat. I shall carry out your plan.

REVEREND PAT: *My* plan? Which was—

TAMMIE: Persuasion. (*She exits.*)

ROSY: I need to speak to you.

REVEREND PAT: I think your friend has gone completely
bonkers, Rosy.

ROSY: That is not unusual for her.

REVEREND PAT: No, I believe she's dangerous. She
thinks she's seeing aliens.

ROSY: Oh, she's been going on about that for years.
Now do I have your attention?

REVEREND PAT: My atten…yes, yes, now what's so important, Miss Rosy? Come sit over here.

(REVEREND PAT *indicates his lap.* ROSY *remains standing.*)

ROSY: I said I would go to the Bahamas with you because you said it's what Jesus wanted.

REVEREND PAT: That is correct, my little praline.

ROSY: But I have been filing the bills, and I see that our tickets and hotel in the Bahamas are on the church account.

REVEREND PAT: Well, aren't you efficient, doing all my filing—

ROSY: On the church account, I said. That means the tithes of our members are paying for—paying for—

REVEREND PAT: Sweetness, I'm gonna tell you something…the Lord has provided the giving of tithes for *us* in a sense, so that *we* may revel in his glory. Let me ask you, what do you think the weekly offering is for?

ROSY: For—for the church. To help people who…poor people—

REVEREND PAT: Oh well, helping people is all very well and good, and we do that at the church. We help poor people plenty. They would be in some sad shape if we did not help them, but let me tell you what it says in Deuteronomy about the tithe. "Thou shalt eat before the Lord, in the place which *he shall choose,* the tithe of thy corn, thy wine, and of thy oil." That's what He said. He's choosing the place…and *we* partake of the tithe *ourselves,* so that we may celebrate him. And the tithe isn't just livestock and oil and produce. No, no, no. "Then shalt thou turn it into money and spend that money…*on whatever thy soul desireth.*" Now you *know* what my soul desireth.

ROSY: It says all that in the Bible?

REVEREND PAT: That's in Deuteronomy, Chapter 14. You can look it up. Now, we are celebrating the glory of the Lord in the place of His choosing. Honey pie, I know in my heart of hearts that the Lord chooseth the Bahamas. How do I know? Because it is the place that I desireth. You do want to go with me, don't you?

ROSY: Yes.

REVEREND PAT: Of course you do. Now come sit on my lap.

(ROSY *sits on* REVEREND PAT's *lap.*)

REVEREND PAT: I think I feel the power of the Lord.

ROSY: *(Sincerely)* I think I feel it too.

*(The lights slowly fade to black. End of scene)*

## Scene 4

### Hardware

*(Setting: A hardware store—Glenehinkel's Hardware. Saturday morning.)*

*(At rise:* LES GLENEHINKEL *[Actor G], the chauvinistic owner of the hardware store is waiting on* TAMMIE.*)*

TAMMIE: *(Frustrated)* So you got nothin'—no kinda tool like that you can sell me?

LES: Do yerself a favor and hire a locksmith, Tammie.

TAMMIE: I don't want a locksmith. Do you sell those thangs?

LES: You don't even know what it's called, Tammie Lynn! How you expect to use a tool you don't even know the name to?

TAMMIE: *(Releasing in frustration)*
AaaaAAAAAHHHhhhhhHHHH. *(Presenting the
crowbar)* This. Can I buy this? It's a crowbar. See, I
know the name and everything.

LES: Well, this ain't a very good crowbar.

TAMMIE: *(About to lose it)* Just sell me the crowbar.

LES: Lessee…seventeen ninety-five, plus tax…that'd
be…

*(As LES figures in his head, TAMMIE becomes impatient,
slaps a twenty on the counter.)*

TAMMIE: Keep the change.

*(TAMMIE grabs her crowbar and is about to leave. ED enters
the store at the same time. She recoils—even audibly—at the
sight of him and goes running from the store.)*

LES: Women should not be allowed in hardware stores,
Ed.

ED: Yep.

LES: That Tammie Lynn Schnieder…I know she's
gettin' hitched to your buddy, but she's not playing
with a full game board, my friend. Know what she
wanted? She wanted, and I quote, "Some kind of
device where I can break into a truck." Women, always
lockin' their damn keys in their vehicles.

ED: Yep.

LES: What I can do you for, Kemosabe?

ED: A saw. I need a heavy duty kind of jig saw.

LES: Oh yeah, we got some beauties in the other day.
What're you gonna be cutting my friend?

ED: It's like an outer covering, a thick, shell-like
covering—

LES: —aluminum siding? I'm not sure—

ED: —well, no, it's hard, it's a thick hard shell, almost petrified it seems.

LES: Hmmmm, so you haven't even really scratched the surface of this baby. Maybe you oughtta just take a crowbar to this—this—wall and rip it down.

ED: No, I've got to be careful. I don't want to damage—

LES: You got some wiring you're not sure about?

ED: Well, I'm afraid my laser's broken.

LES: Yer laser?

(CHUCKY *[Actor T] enters.* LES *should tease* CHUCKY, *but it's not totally mean. They've done this dance before.*)

LES: What do you want, you little loser?

CHUCKY: What's your problem, old man?

LES: Hey Ed, you know this little homo's from up north? Look at that earring he wears. Just like a little girl.

CHUCKY: Hey, I can take my money elsewhere.

LES: Nobody needs yer Yankee money, boy. Hey Ed, I tell you how we had this boy going when he first moved here? We told him the Great Pecan was real. Told him it was real, and this little peckerwood bought it.

CHUCKY: Yeah, yeah, yeah.

ED: You mean it's not real?

LES: Ha, ha, very good, Ed. Yeah, it's reeeeal. Right, Chucky? It's jesta big 'ole juicy nut inside.

ED: Well, what's the Pecan made of then?

LES: Ha, ha. That's just what he asked me, Ed. This ditzy little cow pie couldn't even figure out that Pecan was made of pure concrete. Why it must weigh five hunerd pound.

CHUCKY: I wish I could stay forever down here at hick central, but I do have a lot on the agenda today. If I could just purchase some fertilizer and be on my way.

LES: What are you growing, city boy? You a farmer now? Last I heard you was a rancher—startin' yer own *bull* ranch.

CHUCKY: I'm making a bomb, and I heard fertilizer was what I needed.

LES: What're you gonna blow up?

CHUCKY: I gotta get rid of some stumps in my back yard.

LES: Why don't you just buy some dynamite, boy, and make it easy on yerself?

CHUCKY: You'd sell me dynamite?

LES: Sure. Pull on around back, and I'll have Lenny load you up.

CHUCKY: Th-thanks.

LES: Well, that boy is learning. You know the last five times I asked him, he said Alaska was the biggest state. Really annoyed the hell outta me.

ED: I gotta go, Les.

LES: Well, what about that wall we gotta get down, pardner?

ED: I made a mistake, Les. I'm leaving the shell on.

LES: Just gonna sheet rock right on over that sucker. I got cha. That's an option.

ED: Bye, Les.

LES: All right then, Ed. Hey, hey, hey, Ed, don't go spreading this around, but Sonja talked me into being one of them judges for that there Pecan Beauty Contest. What we do for a little somethin' somethin' on the side, eh Ed?

ED: I gotta go, Les. *(He tries to leave.)*

LES: Hey, hey, hey, Ed. I heard a rumor that they may cancel the Pecan Festival. That does not bode well for me, my friend. Bad for business...and bad for the ole love life. Know what I mean?

ED: All right then, Les. *(He leaves.)*

LES: *(Shouting after him)* All right then. Come on back anytime and shoot the shit, Ed. Don't have to have a reason. See ya later!

*(The lights fade to black. End of scene)*

## Scene 5

## Slamming Doors

*(Four actor version of final scene)*

*(Author's note: This is the four actor version of the last scene. This version eliminates SONJA from the climax of the play, so no more than four performers are on stage at any one time. The virtuosity of each performer will be challenged as they quickly enter and exit as different characters. The "large cast version" of this scene will follow directly.)*

*(Setting: Sonja's Beauty Parlor. Saturday morning)*

*(At rise: SONJA [Actor R], has just finished a trim on REVEREND PAT [Actor E]. She shows him the back of his head in a mirror. This is a quick change for Actor E. In this scene practically every character makes a brief appearance. In certain portions the scene should be reminiscent of a French farce with people running in and out of slamming doors.)*

REVEREND PAT: Oh that's just lovely, dear. Lovely. Have to look sharp for my duties on the Jesus float.

SONJA: Does Jesus look like a giant piñata again?

REVEREND PAT: No, the youth group has done some amazing things with papier-mâché this year.

(SONJA *leans over the instrument cart.* REVEREND PAT *can't help but to check out her rear-end.*)

REVEREND PAT: So when are we going to see your lovely face back in church again, my dear?

SONJA: Well, you might not wanna hole your breath on that one Revrend Pat.

(GREELEY *[Actor G] enters out of breath. This is a quick change for Actor G.*)

GREELEY: Where's Tammie? (*Noticing* REVEREND PAT *and shuffling nervously*) Oh, hey, Revrend.

REVEREND PAT: (*Nodding stoically*) Mister Green.

GREELEY: You know where Tammie is?

SONJA: Late as usual. And she's got an eleven o'clock appointment with Mrs Sheriff.

GREELEY: See the thing is…my truck is gone. I had it parked right out here in front of my Mom's store. Now there's just an empty spot and a mess-a windshield glass.

SONJA: Somebody stole jer truck?

REVEREND PAT: Heavens.

GREELEY: Well, I think…I dunno. I do know that Tammie bought a crowbar at Glenehinkel's Hardware. (*Short beat*) I, I, I have to go to the sheriff. Or…maybe I should wait and find Tammie. What do you think I should do?

SONJA: Wait for Tammie.

GREELEY: Yeah. Okay. I'll be at the nursery.

SONJA: Come back later for a trim, Greeley. Your head is like an unruly garden.

(GREELEY *exits.*)

SONJA: He never lets Tammie cut his hair. Is a very bad sign for marriage.

(MRS ROTTWEILER *[Actor T] comes in.*)

MRS ROTTWEILER: Hello, are you Sonja?

SONJA: You got me.

MRS ROTTWEILER: Oh, Revrend Pat, well, I guess if you come to this salon it must be good.

REVEREND PAT: Yes, indeed, Mrs. Rottweiler, Sonja is the best barber in town.

SONJA: *Gracias*, Revrend Pat.

MRS ROTTWEILER: Well, I heard about you on the radio, Sonja. My daughter is in the car and is really down in the dumps because she had her heart all set on competing in this year's Pecan Queen contest. I think she's just in desperate need of a little pampering—maybe a facial, a manicure. If I can coax her out of the car, could you fit her in today?

SONJA: Today is your lucky day. Bring her in.

MRS ROTTWEILER: Oh good. My goodness, is that a poster of Mel Gibson? That is just scrumptious.

(LES *[Actor G] pops his head in.*)

LES: You girls have any quarters?

SONJA: No, I don't have no quarters. Do I look like a slot machine?

LES: I got something for yer slot machine. How's about I give you a big kiss? Will you give me some quarters then?

SONJA: I'll cut you in quarters, thas' what I'll do. Go sell some hammers.

LES: You are one hot tamale. Well, you know where to find me. *(He leaves.)*

SONJA: *Pendejo.* Sorry, Revrend Pat.

REVEREND PAT: I don't know how you put up with these cretins, Sonja. You are an angel.

MRS ROTTWEILER: Did you see *Lethal Weapon?* He is so cute.

REVEREND PAT: This is for you, my dear.

SONJA: Oh Revrend, a whole dollar tip. I don't even know what to say.

REVEREND PAT: Well, I wish it could be more, but we messengers of the Lord lead a simple life.

SONJA: Yeah, I'm surprised you can afford a thirty dollar hair cut.

REVEREND PAT: One of my few luxuries. Ladies. See you in church. *(He exits.)*

MRS ROTTWEILER: He is such a handsome man.

SONJA: He's got good hair.

*(FRANCIO [Actor G] enters.)*

FRANCIO: Hello, baby.

SONJA: How you doin', baby?

FRANCIO: I'm okay, baby. Was that the holy man?

SONJA: *Si.*

FRANCIO: He don't like me.

SONJA: Why not, baby?

FRANCIO: He say I'm going to *el diablo, porque no me gustan las chicas.*

SONJA: You don't like me, baby?

FRANCIO: Like a sister, baby. Will you give me *il permanente?*

SONJA: Now what chew want with that? You don't got enough trouble?

FRANCIO: I got to be me, baby.

SONJA: Okay, I'll tell you what. I got to go get some quarters for that *porco* next door. He may be an asshole, but he's the only date I got right now.

FRANCIO: You and that hardware man? Oooooo.

MRS ROTTWEILER: Do you mind if I just rest my feet for a bit? It is so peaceful in here.

SONJA: Take a load off, Miss. *(To* FRANCIO*)* Will you keep an eye on the shop for a few minutes?

FRANCIO: You want me to watch the salon?

SONJA: *Por favor.*

FRANCIO: I am honored, Sonja…*honored.*

SONJA: It ain't no big deal. I'll be right back, miss. *(She exits.)*

FRANCIO: You come in for a perm, miss?

MRS ROTTWEILER: No, no, my daughter is getting— getting made over. She's just pouting in the car at the moment.

*(*ED *[Actor E] comes in—more disheveled than we've ever seen him.)*

ED: Excuse me. A Miss Tammie Lynn Schneider works in this parlor, doesn't she?

FRANCIO: Tammie ain't here yet.

ED: Oh. But she works here?

FRANCIO: Last I checked.

ED: It's important I speak to her. She's been talking around town, you see. Things are getting out of hand. When is she expected?

FRANCIO: Uh, Sonja will be back in a few minutes.

(PRISCILLA *[Actor R] still wearing her evening gown—
bursts through the door.* MRS ROTTWEILER, *who was
meditating in a chair, eyes closed, jumps to the roof upon
hearing her voice.*)

PRISCILLA: Mother, for God's sake! Can we please go?

FRANCIO: Where's the party, baby?

ED: Excuse me. *(He exits quickly.)*

MRS ROTTWEILER: Priscilla, honey, I was just waiting
for the lady to come back. She said she can give you a
nice facial and a manicure.

PRISCILLA: I do not want a facial. I do not want a
manicure. I want to go home.

MRS ROTTWEILER: I just thought this would make you
feel better, honey.

PRISCILLA: I do not want to feel better. I want to feel
what I feel, until they catch the person who did what
he did.

FRANCIO: A facial will make you feel better, baby.

MRS ROTTWEILER: Mommy will get one too.

PRISCILLA: There's something dreadfully paradoxical
about getting a facial when one is on a hunger strike.

MRS ROTTWEILER: Honey, are you still on that hunger
strike? I thought those chocolate chip pancakes kinda
canceled that out.

PRISCILLA: Is that Mel Gibson?

FRANCIO: You got it, baby.

(SHERIFF BART *[Actor E] enters.*)

SHERIFF BART: *(Nodding to the ladies)* Ladies. *(Then to
FRANCIO)* Are you Francio?

FRANCIO: *(Saluting him)* Mister Sheriff!

SHERIFF BART: That—that won't be necessary. I need to talk to you.

FRANCIO: To me? You need to talk to Francio?

MRS ROTTWEILER: Well, if you'll excuse us Sheriff, we were just leaving.

SHERIFF BART: Now I didn't mean to scare you ladies off. This business should just take a few minutes.

MRS ROTTWEILER: No, we were on our way.

PRISCILLA: When will you catch the Pecan thief, Sheriff?

SHERIFF BART: Oh we'll catch him, Missy, don't you worry your pretty lil' head about that.

PRISCILLA: I hope you hurt him, Sheriff. I hope you hurt him as he's hurt me.

SHERIFF BART: We will deal with him as soundly as the law allows us.

PRISCILLA: I wish I could catch him.

MRS ROTTWEILER: *(Leading her by the arm)* Priscilla, let's get home and take that medication.

PRISCILLA: I would tear his eye balls out.

MRS ROTTWEILER: Come along, dear.

*(MRS ROTTWEILER and PRISCILLA exit.)*

SHERIFF BART: Strange child.

FRANCIO: Yes, Mister Sheriff.

SHERIFF BART: Now Francio, I know you hang out 'round the town square in the wee hours of the mornin'.

FRANCIO: No, not me, Sheriff. I go to bed early.

SHERIFF BART: I know that ain't true, Francio. I'm not here ta get chew in any sorta trouble. I jes' want to know if you saw anythang the night the Great Pecan was stolen.

FRANCIO: Mister Sheriff, I know your wife. She come in here all the time.

SHERIFF BART: Yes, too damn much if you ask me.

FRANCIO: She's a nice lady.

SHERIFF BART: She's a she-wolf from hell, Francio. Now did you see anythang strange in the wee hours of the night in question—October 15th—last Saturday night inta Sunday mornin'?

FRANCIO: Oh no, I was in bed by ten.

SHERIFF BART: Yer not makin' this easy, boy. You know this could go as smooth as silk pie.

(ROSY [Actor R] enters in a hurry.)

ROSY: They told me you'd be here, Sheriff Bart.

SHERIFF BART: You're looking for me, sweetie?

ROSY: I had something to talk to you about.

SHERIFF BART: Okay, Rosy. Just one second. (To FRANCIO) You got nothing else ta say ta me, fancy pants?

FRANCIO: I wish I could help you, Mister Sheriff.

SHERIFF BART: Hmmphhh. You think of anythang, anythang at all, you give me a call. (To ROSY) Now what is it, Rosy?

ROSY: Uh, well, do you mind coming over here?

FRANCIO: Don't mind me. I'm just watching the store for Sonja.

ROSY: This is a little bit embarrassing. You see, I've been seeing Revrend Pat. Well, he's married, so it isn't like I'm seeing him, but—

SHERIFF BART: I think I know what you mean, dear.

ROSY: Well, I do his books, you know, and we was going to the Bahamas together, and he told me it was all right for the church to pay, but I told him it wasn't, but he convinced me cuz of Deuteronomy, Chapter 14, and I even looked it up, but then I found the other things like some bank account with a million dollars in the Cayman Islands, and it just didn't seem right somehow, a man of God with a million dollars, so I decided to come to you first and ask you what to do.

SHERIFF BART: Right, right. And yer wondering how he got all that money?

ROSY: Sheriff, he drives a purple B M W.

SHERIFF BART: I do believe you are right.

ROSY: Yeah, thas' an expensive car, I think.

SHERIFF BART: Caymer Islands. Well, if that don't beat the cake.

ROSY: Did I do the right thang?

SHERIFF BART: Yes you did, darling.

(CHUCKY [Actor T] sticks his head in.)

CHUCKY: Hey, Sheriff—

SHERIFF BART: What do you want, boy?

CHUCKY: Nothing. Just saw you in the window, and I thought I'd say "hi". Any luck on that Pecan caper?

SHERIFF BART: Go on about yer bidness, son. I don't have time for nonsense today.

(CHUCKY enters all the way.)

CHUCKY: Don't have time for me today, huh? Well, hardy har har.

SHERIFF BART: Come on, Rosy. Let's go straighten this out with the Revrend.

(ROSY and SHERIFF BART exit)

CHUCKY: Good to see you, Sheriff. *(To* FRANCIO*)* You know, I would like to shake the hand of the person who stole that Pecan.

FRANCIO: I was in bed by ten, baby.

CHUCKY: I mean, the bull semen heist seems like an amateurish prank in comparison to the raw havoc that missing Pecan has wrought upon this pathetic little town. I would bow down and grovel at the feet of the Pecan Thief if I met him. You know what I mean?

FRANCIO: I know. Kiss his feet. If he had his toe nails done, I would probably kiss his feet too, baby.

CHUCKY: Freak. I gotta get outta here.

FRANCIO: You want a manicure, baby? A facial? I can pop those zits for jou.

*(*SONJA *[Actor R] enters.)*

SONJA: I'm baaaack. Can I help you?

CHUCKY: Yeah, put me down for a zit popping tomorrow at four. Later, girls. *(He exits.)*

FRANCIO: Don't take him serious.

SONJA: Everything okay while I was gone? Where did that lady go?

FRANCIO: Her daughter didn't want no facial. And I didn't do nothing.

SONJA: Okay, baby. Still no Mrs. Bart?

*(*MRS BART *[Actor E] enters.)*

MRS BART: Here I am. Here I am. Sorry I'm late, girls. Oh, hello, uh, Francio. I didn't know—

FRANCIO: Thas all right.

SONJA: Francio, jer *permanente* will have to wait, okay? Cuz I got no Tammie right now.

FRANCIO: Thas all right, baby. I'll come back later.

SONJA: Come around five o'clock. I'll fix jou up *muy bonita*.

FRANCIO: Later, baby. *(He leaves.)*

SONJA: Later. Well, Mrs Sheriff. Can you stand to have me instead of Tammie?

MRS BART: Actually, I would prefer to have you today. Apparently, Tammie has been seen driving a truck around town with a big, huge sign that says, "ED HAS THE PECAN, AND HE'S FROM OUTERSPACE."

SONJA: *Ay, dios mio.*

MRS BART: She is on the verge of some sort of breakdown. I almost didn't come today for fear she'd ruin my hair. I've heard she intends to drive that inflammatory sign through the parade.

SONJA: There must be some esplanation, Mrs. Bart.

MRS BART: I have to look my best today, Sonja. I'm covering the Pecan Queen Pageant for the *Gazette* tonight…that is, assuming there still is a pageant—

*(TAMMIE [Actor T] throws the door open and stands in the middle of it. She is completely disheveled—torn clothing, dirt on her face and arms, hair like a rat's nest, a shotgun in hand, but she keeps an emphatically calm facade as if nothing were out of the ordinary. One senses she might burst like a cracked dam at any moment.)*

TAMMIE: Sorry I'm late, Sonja. Hello, Mrs Bart.

MRS BART & SONJA: *(Attempting cheerfulness)* Hello.

TAMMIE: I'm ready for your styling, Mrs Bart. Just give me one moment to collect my instruments.

MRS BART: Take your time, dear.

SONJA: No rush.

MRS BART: I'm actually having second thoughts about my hair today. In a bit of a hurry, you know.

TAMMIE: Now, Mrs Bart, I insist. Your hair is in a shambles.

MRS BART: *(Looking at* TAMMIE's *hair in bewilderment)* Is it?

TAMMIE: You just leave it to me. Today's a big day.

SONJA: Tammie, you okay, *chica?*

TAMMIE: Of course I'm okay...oh, you mean the shotgun. Haven't you ever heard of a shotgun wedding?

MRS BART: Uh—

TAMMIE: Me and Greeley. He'll be here soon. You'll see. He'll be looking for his truck, and when he gets here... *(She holds up the shotgun.)* We're getting married.

SONJA: Tammie, honey, this ain't the way to get a husband.

MRS BART: I'm afraid I'll have to be leaving—

TAMMIE: NOBODY LEAVES!!! *(Pumping the shotgun)* Today we're gonna have a wedding.

*(*GREELEY *[Actor G] enters. He doesn't immediately comprehend what's going on.)*

GREELEY: Where's my truck? Uh...hello? What's with the shotgun?

*(*TAMMIE *points the shotgun at* GREELEY.*)*

TAMMIE: Gitcher ass over here, Greeley! Mrs Bart, go fetch Revrend Pat.

MRS BART: Yes, of course.

TAMMIE: Sorry about yer appointment. We'll reschedule for tomorrow.

MRS BART: Not a problem, dear. First things first. *(She exits.)*

GREELEY: My truck better be all right.

TAMMIE: Yer truck. Yer truck. Thas' all I hear about is yer truck. You do what I say today, or you'll never see that truck again. You understand, Greeley Green?

GREELEY: Yeah, I understand.

SONJA: *(Sitting down)* Go ahead, Greeley. Take a load off.

GREELEY: I have to go to the toilet.

TAMMIE: Yeah, fat chance.

GREELEY: I'm not lying. I have to go. I had Mexican for lunch. Look, if I don't come back, you can shoot Sonja.

SONJA: *Pendejo.*

TAMMIE: Yeah, okay, but I'm watching you.

*(GREELEY exits to the bathroom.)*

TAMMIE: There ain't any windows in there, right?

SONJA: No. *(Beat)* I hope it works out for you, Tammie, but it seems like a long shot to me.

TAMMIE: It's gonna work out.

*(DIGGITY [Actor G] sticks his head only in the front door.)*

DIGGITY: Sheriff Bart here yet?

TAMMIE: What? DIGGITY!

DIGGITY: Sheriff Bart here?

TAMMIE: No!

DIGGITY: You jes' wait 'til he gits here. Don't shoot anybody yet.

TAMMIE: Get the hell outta here, Diggity. Go get Revrend Pat.

*(DIGGITY exits.)*

TAMMIE: Damn ignoramus.

SONJA: He's got a little, tiny pencil dick.

TAMMIE: What???

SONJA: I heard.

*(The voice of* SHERIFF BART *comes over a megaphone from outside.)*

SHERIFF BART: *(O S)* Okay, Tammie, we know yer in there.

TAMMIE: *(Going to the door and yelling out)* Yeah, okay, good. Now where's the Revrend? *(Towards the bathroom)* Greeley, you still in there?

GREELEY: Yes.

SHERIFF BART: *(O S)* This is pointless, Tammie. I got three stations from the San Antonia news out here with cameras. You know I can't put the Revrend in harm's way. Yer gonna hafta let those hostages go.

TAMMIE: Ain't gonna happen Sheriff. One of two things will take place today. A bloodbath or a weddin'. You decide.

SHERIFF BART: *(O S)* Look, Tammie, the Revrend's on his way. Don't you go doin' anythang half cocked.

TAMMIE: Hey, Sheriff, I got a deal for you. You send that Revrend in here, and I'll tell you where the Great Pecan is hiding.

SHERIFF BART: *(O S)* Whudda you know about the Great Pecan, Tammie?

TAMMIE: I didn't take it, but I know who did. *(Towards the bathroom)* Greeley?

GREELEY: *(O S)* Tammie, you cain't rush these things.

SHERIFF BART: *(O S)* So why don't you tell me, Missy?

TAMMIE: Do we have a wedding?

SHERIFF BART: *(O S)* On one condition. You send out Sonja.

SONJA: Oh no, no, no. I gotta see the end of this.

TAMMIE: Come on, Sonja, *por favor.*

SONJA: *(Getting up)* You better take some pictures of the wedding.

TAMMIE: Sonja's coming out. The Great Pecan is at Ed's house on 123 Bypass. He's using it in some kinda weird naked alien ritual deal.

SONJA: *(Kissing her on the cheek)* Okay, good luck, honey. Lock up when jer done.

TAMMIE: Thank you, Sonja.

*(SONJA exits and GREELEY comes out of the bathroom.)*

GREELEY: Can I go too?

TAMMIE: YOU STAY PUT!!!

SHERIFF BART: *(O S)* Okay, Tammie, I'm sending my deputy to check out yer story. And now the Revrend's here. He's agreed to come in. Don't shoot him. I repeat: *do not shoot him.*

TAMMIE: Send him in.

GREELEY: I don't have a—a ring.

*(TAMMIE pulls out some keys on a ring.)*

TAMMIE: Here, we'll use this key ring.

GREELEY: Thas' ma spare set.

TAMMIE: Yep. How you think I got yer truck started? Got them out of yer glove compartment after I busted up yer window.

GREELEY: My—my window?

*(REVEREND PAT [Actor E] enters.)*

REVEREND PAT: Well, here I am. Let's get this over with. I've got a plane to catch. Duty calls in other ports. But I promised the Sheriff I'd do this before I depart.

TAMMIE: Let's get to it, Revrend.

REVEREND PAT: Would be nice to have a witness, but let's—

*(Enter* ROSY *[Actor R])*

ROSY: I'll witness it Revrend Pat.

REVEREND PAT: Well, well, well.

TAMMIE: Rosy!

*(They hug.)*

TAMMIE: I'm finally gonna get married, honey. *(To* REVEREND PAT*)* She's my maid of honor.

REVEREND PAT: Very well.

ROSY: Let's do it before they send in the SWAT team.

GREELEY: I think I gotta go to the bathroom again.

TAMMIE: *(Waving the gun)* Get over here. There'll be plenty-uh time for that later.

REVEREND PAT: *(Nervous at the sight of the gun—rushing through)* Dearly beleaguered we are gathered here today to join these three in holy matrimoooony. Do you Greeley take this woman Rosy—

TAMMIE & ROSY: —Tammie!

REVEREND PAT: Tam—Rose—Tammie to be yer lawful wedded wife to have and to hold 'til—'til—'til—

TAMMIE & ROSY: —death!

REVEREND PAT: —death, I say, death, do you part?

GREELEY: Yeah, I mean, what choice do I have?

REVEREND PAT: Tammie, Tammie, do you take this man Reilley—

TAMMIE & ROSY: —Greeley!

REVEREND PAT: —Greeley, to be yer awful wedded husband, to have and to hold from this day forth 'til death [uh] do you part!

TAMMIE: I do.

REVEREND PAT: Then by the power vested in me, I now pronounce you man and wife. You may now kiss the bride. Mind the gun barrel.

(TAMMIE *kisses* GREELEY.)

REVEREND PAT: Well, the time has come to say good-bye.

(REVEREND PAT *is about to leave, but then as a last thought, he dips* ROSY *into a kiss.*)

REVEREND PAT: Rosy, it could have been great in the Bahamas. *Adieu. (He exits.)*

TAMMIE: Yer truck is parked over at the El Burro restaurant `round the back.

GREELEY: And it's okay?

TAMMIE: Except for a broken windshield, it's fine. I'll replace it.

GREELEY: If you wanted to get married this bad, why didn't you just say so?

TAMMIE: Greeley, I'm gonna strangle you.

SHERIFF BART: *(O S)* Tammie, Tammie, is everything all right in there?

TAMMIE: Yeah, Sheriff.

SHERIFF BART: *(O S)* Look, Tammie, why don't you let me come in there? I think we can work this thang out. The media is gone. Sonja ain't gonna press no charges.

TAMMIE: Okay, come on in.

GREELEY: Can I go to the bathroom now?

TAMMIE: Jes' say hi to Sheriff Bart first.

(SHERIFF BART *[Actor E] enters—not nervous about the gun in the least.*)

SHERIFF BART: Everybody all right in here?

GREELEY: I still gotta go to the bathroom.

TAMMIE: Go...*go!*

(GREELEY *quickly exits.*)

SHERIFF BART: You wanna give me that pea shooter, Tammie?

TAMMIE: It ain't loaded.

SHERIFF BART: I know it ain't, Missy.

(DIGGITY *[Actor G] sticks his head in the door.*)

DIGGITY: Sheriff? Sheriff Bart. Oh, hi Tammie. Congratulations on yer marriage. I bought you a toaster.

SHERIFF BART: What is it, Diggity?

DIGGITY: We got a pretty ugly situation over't Ed's house. That Rottweiler girl is leading an angry lynch mob over there now. They're callin' for the head of the man who stole the Great Pecan. The news stations from San Antonia are over there too. It's on the T V right now.

SHERIFF BART: Okay, round up everybody, and let's get over there pronto.

DIGGITY: Yes, Sheriff.

(DIGGITY *exits.* ROSY *makes her way over to the t.v. and turns it on—flipping stations*)

SHERIFF BART: Tammie, I'm gonna trust you to come down to the station tomorrow. I'm gonna hafta come up with some kinda charges.

TAMMIE: I know, Sheriff.

SHERIFF BART: No more shenanigans for tonight.

*(GREELEY re-enters.)*

GREELEY: Sheriff, what about me?

SHERIFF BART: You're free to go, Greeley.
Congratulations on your marriage.

GREELEY: Congratulations…but…

*(SHERIFF BART exits in a hurry. On the television, all pre-taped on video using a bit of green screen, PRISCILLA is speaking to a newscaster, KITTY ST CLAIR.)*

ROSY: Look, it's on the T V!

KITTY ST CLAIR: *(On T V)* Thank you, Bill, we are out here on 123 Bypass outside the barn of a man known in Seguin only as "Ed". Apparently, we have no last name for him. This Ed is holed up inside the barn, and an angry crowd is starting to gather with calls of "string him up", and "dirty pecan thief", and "I've got a rope in my truck". If you want to put a human face on the kind of pain this man has cause by allegedly stealing the Great Pecan, you need go no further than high school senior, Priscilla Rottweiller.

*(PRISCILLA steps aggressively into the camera.)*

PRISCILLA: I'm here to represent all of the young girls who won't be able to compete for Pecan Queen this year because of this evil man. He deserves the strictest punishment our law allows. Now that we've caught him, and now that justice *will* prevail, perhaps after time and intense therapy the wounds may heal.

KITTY ST CLAIR: *(On T V)* Well, there you have it, Bill, this angry mob is ready to explode at any moment…

*(There is a loud explosion, almost like a rocket ignition. The barn collapses.)*

KITTY ST CLAIR: *(On T V)* Wait, what's that? Oh my gosh, it looks like the barn's just exploded. Did you get that?

ROSY: Oh dear Lord.

GREELEY: ED!

CHUCKY: *(On T V)* I blew it up! I did it! Free the space man! Don't put him in a test tube! FREEEEEDOM!

GREELEY: Is that that Yankee kid, Chucky?

KITTY ST CLAIR: *(On T V)* Sorry, Bill, there are some bad apples in the crowd.

*(There is an otherworldy sound.)*

KITTY ST CLAIR: *(On T V)* Oh dear Lord, rising from the rubble, Bill, are you seeing this? It looks like some, some kind of aircraft, or space craft…oh Sweet Jesus… hovering—just hovering in the sky. Tell me you are getting this!

*(GREELEY, ROSY and TAMMIE are all about to go outside. Cut to stock footage of space ship, then the T V goes blank for a second before ED comes on the screen. He is speaking from his spaceship. They all stop in their tracks.)*

ED: Greetings earthlings and Texans.

ROSY: Oh my Lord.

TAMMIE: I told ya he was an alien!

ED: I thought our mutual coexistence was an experiment that could work. Your planet has a wealth of the valuable *pecan,* which we use on our world for fuel, sustenance, and tanning oil.

GREELEY: *(Forlorn)* Ed!

ED: I admit I crossed the boundaries of proper intergalactic etiquette when I took your sacred shrine. I saw it falling into disrepair, saw the grey rat-birds leave the liquidy white excrement upon it, saw the young pubescent beings spray it with ozone damaging methylene chloride based dyes. I thought you had forsaken your sacred icon.

TAMMIE: It's true the T V does add ten pounds.

ED: I was not prepared for the mosaic of beautiful human emotions at its disappearance. I saw the pecan as a product for profitable resale on my world and not as the spiritual, mystical beacon which your people obviously believe it to be. Therefore, I am returning the Great Pecan to you with my sincerest apologies.

ROSY: Oh thank Jesus! The Festival is saved!

ED: I dare not make another landing lest I incur your further ire, but I will now release the Great Pecan with a parachute to fetter its descent. With sorrow I take my leave of you, and I particularly will miss the one called Greeley—

GREELEY: Ed!

ED: —who was a good friend. In the language of my people...*preHHHHa brrreej Greeley-neeshhh.* Until we meet again.

*(The T V goes blank.)*

ROSY: It ain't workin' anymore.

TAMMIE: Let's try the radio.

*(ROSY turns on the radio.)*

JOHNNY JOHNS: *(V O)* —can all see the Great Pecan now as it glides down to the earth. It looks like it's headed toward 123 Bypass. Police and State Troopers have cleared off the highways... Oh, wait, there's one lone car on the highway who's apparently broken through the police barrier. It appears to be a purple B M W. He does not see the descending pecan, and, oh my God, they appear to be on a direct collision course. Somebody's got to stop that car. *(Overlapping)* He just doesn't seem to realize what's been going on.

ROSY: *(Overlapping)* Oh dear Lord, I still love him...

*(ROSY and TAMMIE hug.)*

JOHNNY JOHNS: *(V O)* Oh! Oh my! He's been hit.

(ROSY *gasps.*)

JOHNNY JOHNS: *(V O)* He's been hit by the Great Pecan! The car has been literally squashed by the great weight of the Pecan. If anyone is alive in there, it would be a miracle…a miracle.

ROSY: I can't take it.

JOHNNY JOHNS: *(V O)* We're now being told that the car belongs to Revrend Pat of the Third Baptist Church. The police are racing toward him now. If you're just joining us, an alien spaceship just dropped the Great Pecan out of the sky, and it has landed on Revrend Pat of the Third Baptist Church. There's Sheriff Bart now. He's looking inside the car.

ROSY: Oh, for the love of God!

JOHNNY JOHNS: *(V O)* He's giving us the thumbs up! I say he's giving us the thumbs up.

(ROSY *and* TAMMIE *cheer.* GREELEY *could take it or leave it.*)

JOHNNY JOHNS: *(V O)* I'm quite sure the jaws of life will be needed to excavate the Revrend from the wreckage, but at least we know that he's alive.

ROSY: Thank you, Jesus.

JOHNNY JOHNS: *(V O)* This is Johnny Johns. This has been the noon traffic report. *(Beat)* Okay, let's switch gears here a little. We gotta send a big ole congratulations to Tammie Lynn Schneider and Greeley Green who finally tied the knot. They were married today in a private ceremony over't Sonja's Beauty Parlor. They're registered over't Horner's Department store if you want to send a gift.

GREELEY: We're registered?!

JOHNNY JOHNS: *(V O)* This next song goes out to Mister and Mrs Greeley Green. All the best y'all.

*(A country song plays on the radio.)*

ROSY: Scuse me. I'll just go freshen up. *(She exits.)*

TAMMIE: Shall we go get your truck, Greeley?

GREELEY: I don't know what the hell is going on today.

TAMMIE: You wanna go to the Dixie Drive-In tonight? I think there's a double feature: *Mad Max Beyond Thunderdome* and *E T.*

GREELEY: Yeah, okay.

TAMMIE: Can we bring Rosy along? She's in mourning for the Revrend.

GREELEY: He didn't die.

TAMMIE: Yeah, well he's dead to this town.

GREELEY: Yeah, sure, she can come. *(Quietly, to the heavens)* Ed…

TAMMIE: Here's yer spare set of keys.

GREELEY: Uh, tha's all right. You keep 'em.

TAMMIE: Really?

GREELEY: Yeah, what the hell. You can drive it if you want.

*(TAMMIE is choked up by the gesture. That's all she ever wanted.)*

TAMMIE: I don't really wanna drive it.

GREELEY: What the hell did you steal it for?

TAMMIE: I just wanted you to make the offer.

GREELEY: I WILL NEVER UNDERSTAND WOMEN!

TAMMIE: I love you, Greeley Green.

GREELEY: Yeah, well, I love you too, honey pie.

(GREELEY *and* TAMMIE *kiss.* ROSY *comes to the door and watches them as they dance the Texas Two Step. The lights fade slowly to black.)*

*(End of four actor version of the last scene)*

## END OF PLAY

## Scene 5

## ALTERNATE VERSION

## Slamming Doors

*(Author's note: This is the large cast version of the last scene for more than four actors. The major difference is that it appropriately adds* SONJA *into the final moments of the play.)*

*(Setting: Sonja's Beauty Parlor. Saturday morning)*

*(At rise:* SONJA *[Actor R], has just finished a trim on* REVEREND PAT *[Actor E]. She shows him the back of his head in a mirror. This is a quick change for Actor E. In this scene practically every character makes a brief appearance. In certain portions the scene should be reminiscent of a French farce with people running in and out of slamming doors.)*

REVEREND PAT: Oh that's just lovely, dear. Lovely. Have to look sharp for my duties on the Jesus float.

SONJA: Does Jesus look like a giant piñata again?

REVEREND PAT: No, the youth group has done some amazing things with papier-mâché this year.

*(*SONJA *leans over the instrument cart.* REVEREND PAT *can't help but check out her rear-end.)*

REVEREND PAT: So when are we going to see your lovely face back in church again, my dear?

SONJA: Well, you might not wanna hole your breath on that one Revrend Pat.

*(*GREELEY *[Actor G] enters out of breath.)*

GREELEY: Where's Tammie? *(Noticing* REVEREND PAT *and shuffling nervously)* Oh, hey, Revrend.

REVEREND PAT: *(Nodding stoically)* Mister Green.

GREELEY: You know where Tammie is?

SONJA: Late as usual. And she's got an eleven o'clock appointment with Mrs Sheriff.

GREELEY: See the thing is…my truck is gone. I had it parked right out here in front of my Mom's store. Now there's just an empty spot and a mess-a windshield glass.

SONJA: Somebody stole jer truck?

REVEREND PAT: Heavens.

GREELEY: Well, I think…I dunno. I do know that Tammie bought a crowbar at Glenehinkel's Hardware. *(Short beat)* I, I, I have to go to the sheriff. Or…maybe I should wait and find Tammie?

SONJA: Wait for Tammie.

GREELEY: Yeah. Okay. I'll be at the nursery.

SONJA: Come back later for a trim, Greeley. Your head is like an unruly garden.

(GREELEY *exits.)*

SONJA: He never lets Tammie cut his hair. Is a very bad sign for marriage.

(MRS ROTTWEILER *[Actor T] comes in.)*

MRS ROTTWEILER: Hello, are you Sonja?

SONJA: You got me.

MRS ROTTWEILER: Oh, Revrend Pat, well, I guess if you come to this salon it must be good.

REVEREND PAT: Yes, indeed, Mrs Rottweiler, Sonja is the best barber in town.

SONJA: *Gracias,* Revrend Pat.

MRS ROTTWEILER: Well, I heard about you on the radio, Sonja. My daughter is in the car and is really down in the dumps because she had her heart all set on competing in this year's Pecan Queen contest. I think she's just in desperate need of a little pampering— maybe a facial, a manicure. If I can coax her out of the car, could you fit her in today?

SONJA: Today is your lucky day. Bring her in.

MRS ROTTWEILER: Oh good. My goodness, is that a poster of Mel Gibson? That is just scrumptious.

(MRS ROTTWEILER *crosses to the poster.* LES *[Actor G] pops his head in.)*

LES: You girls have any quarters?

SONJA: No, I don't have no quarters. Do I look like a slot machine?

LES: I got something for yer slot machine. How's about I give you a big kiss? Will you give me some quarters then?

SONJA: I'll cut you in quarters, thas' what I'll do. Go sell some hammers.

LES: You are one hot tamale. Well, you know where to find me. *(He leaves.)*

SONJA: *Pendejo.* Sorry, Revrend Pat.

REVEREND PAT: I don't know how you put up with these cretins, Sonja. You are an angel.

MRS ROTTWEILER: Did you see *Lethal Weapon?* He is so cute.

REVEREND PAT: This is for you, my dear.

SONJA: Oh Revrend, a whole dollar tip. I don't even know what to say.

REVEREND PAT: Well, I wish it could be more, but we messengers of the Lord lead a simple life.

SONJA: Yeah, I'm surprised you can afford a thirty dollar hair cut.

REVEREND PAT: One of my few luxuries. Ladies. See you in church. *(He exits.)*

MRS ROTTWEILER: He is such a handsome man.

SONJA: He's got good hair.

*(FRANCIO [Actor G] enters.)*

FRANCIO: Hello, baby.

SONJA: How you doin', baby?

FRANCIO: I'm okay, baby. Was that the holy man?

SONJA: *Si.*

FRANCIO: He don't like me.

SONJA: Why not, baby?

FRANCIO: He say I'm going to *el diablo, porque no me gustan las chicas.*

SONJA: You don't like me, baby?

FRANCIO: Like a sister, baby. Will you give me *il permanente?*

SONJA: Now what chew want with that? You don't got enough trouble?

FRANCIO: I got to be me, baby.

SONJA: Okay, I'll tell you what. I got to go get some quarters for that *porco* next door. He may be an asshole, but he's the only date I got right now.

FRANCIO: You and that hardware man? Oooooo.

MRS ROTTWEILER: Do you mind if I just rest my feet for a bit? It is so peaceful in here.

SONJA: Take a load off, Miss. *(To FRANCIO)* Will you keep an eye on the shop for a few minutes?

FRANCIO: You want me to watch the salon?

SONJA: *Por favor.*

FRANCIO: I am honored, Sonja...*honored.*

SONJA: It ain't no big deal. I'll be right back, miss. *(She exits.)*

FRANCIO: You come in for a perm, miss?

MRS ROTTWEILER: No, no, my daughter is getting— getting made over. She's just pouting in the car at the moment.

*(ED [Actor E] comes in—more disheveled than we've ever seen him.)*

ED: Excuse me. A Miss Tammie Lynn Schneider works in this parlor, doesn't she?

FRANCIO: Tammie ain't here yet.

ED: Oh. But she works here?

FRANCIO: Last I checked.

ED: It's important I speak to her. She's been talking around town, you see. Things are getting out of hand. When is she expected?

FRANCIO: Uh, Sonja will be back in a few minutes.

*(PRISCILLA [Actor R] still wearing her evening gown— bursts through the door. MRS ROTTWEILER, who was meditating in a chair, eyes closed, jumps to the roof upon hearing her voice.)*

PRISCILLA: Mother, for God's sake! Can we please go?

FRANCIO: Where's the party, baby?

ED: Excuse me. *(He exits quickly.)*

MRS ROTTWEILER: Priscilla, honey, I was just waiting for the lady to come back. She said she can give you a nice facial and a manicure.

PRISCILLA: I do not want a facial. I do not want a manicure. I want to go home.

MRS ROTTWEILER: I just thought this would make you feel better, honey.

PRISCILLA: I do not want to feel better. I want to feel what I feel, until they catch the person who did what he did.

FRANCIO: A facial will make you feel better, baby.

MRS ROTTWEILER: Mommy will get one too.

PRISCILLA: There's something dreadfully paradoxical about getting a facial when one is on a hunger strike.

MRS ROTTWEILER: Honey, are you still on that hunger strike? I thought those chocolate chip pancakes kinda canceled that out.

PRISCILLA: Is that Mel Gibson?

FRANCIO: You got it, baby.

(SHERIFF BART *[Actor E] enters.)*

SHERIFF BART: *(Nodding to the ladies)* Ladies. *(Then to* FRANCIO*)* Are you Francio?

FRANCIO: *(Saluting him)* Mister Sheriff!

SHERIFF BART: That—that won't be necessary. I need to talk to you.

FRANCIO: To me? You need to talk to Francio?

MRS ROTTWEILER: Well, if you'll excuse us Sheriff, we were just leaving.

SHERIFF BART: Now I didn't mean to scare you ladies off. This business should just take a few minutes.

MRS ROTTWEILER: No, we were on our way.

PRISCILLA: When will you catch the Pecan thief, Sheriff?

SHERIFF BART: Oh we'll catch him, Missy, don't you worry your pretty lil' head about that.

PRISCILLA: I hope you hurt him, Sheriff. I hope you hurt him as he's hurt me.

SHERIFF BART: We will deal with him as soundly as the law allows us.

PRISCILLA: I wish I could catch him.

MRS ROTTWEILER: *(Leading her by the arm)* Priscilla, let's get home and take that medication.

PRISCILLA: I would tear his eye balls out.

MRS ROTTWEILER: Come along, dear.

(MRS ROTTWEILER *and* PRISCILLA *exit*)

SHERIFF BART: Strange child.

FRANCIO: Yes, Mister Sheriff.

SHERIFF BART: Now Francio, I know you hang out 'round the town square in the wee hours of the mornin'.

FRANCIO: No, not me, Sheriff. I go to bed early.

SHERIFF BART: I know that ain't true, Francio. I'm not here ta get chew in any sorta trouble. I jes' want to know if you saw anythang the night the Great Pecan was stolen.

FRANCIO: Mister Sheriff, I know your wife. She come in here all the time.

SHERIFF BART: Yes, too damn much if you ask me.

FRANCIO: She's a nice lady.

SHERIFF BART: She's a she-wolf from hell, Francio. Now did you see anythang strange in the wee hours of the night in question—October 15th—last Saturday night inta Sunday mornin'?

FRANCIO: Oh no, I was in bed by ten.

SHERIFF BART: Yer not makin' this easy, boy. You know this could go as smooth as silk pie.

(ROSY [Actor R] enters in a hurry.)

ROSY: They told me you'd be here, Sheriff Bart.

SHERIFF BART: You're looking for me, sweetie?

ROSY: I had something to talk to you about.

SHERIFF BART: Okay, Rosy. Just one second. *(To FRANCIO)* You got nothing else ta say ta me, fancy pants?

FRANCIO: I wish I could help you, Mister Sheriff.

SHERIFF BART: Hmmphhh. You think of anythang, anythang at all, you give me a call. *(To ROSY)* Now what is it, Rosy?

ROSY: Uh, well, do you mind coming over here?

FRANCIO: Don't mind me. I'm just watching the store for Sonja.

ROSY: This is a little bit embarrassing. You see, I've been seeing Revrend Pat. Well, he's married, so it isn't like I'm seeing him, but—

SHERIFF BART: I think I know what you mean, dear.

ROSY: Well, I do his books, you know, and we was going to the Bahamas together, and he told me it was all right for the church to pay, though I told him it wasn't, but he convinced me cuz of Deuteronomy, Chapter 14, and I even looked it up, but then I found the other things like some bank account with a million dollars in the Cayman Islands, and it just didn't seem right somehow, a man of God with a million dollars, so I decided to come to you first and ask you what to do.

SHERIFF BART: Right, right. And yer wondering how he got all that money?

ROSY: Sheriff, he drives a purple B M W.

SHERIFF BART: I do believe you are right.

ROSY: Yeah, thas' an expensive car, I think.

SHERIFF BART: Caymer Islands. Well, if that don't beat the cake.

ROSY: Did I do the right thang?

SHERIFF BART: Yes you did, darling.

(CHUCKY [Actor T] sticks his head in.)

CHUCKY: Hey, Sheriff—

SHERIFF BART: What do you want, boy?

CHUCKY: Nothing. Just saw you in the window, and I thought I'd say "hi". Any luck on that Pecan caper?

SHERIFF BART: Go on about yer bidness, son. I don't have time for nonsense today.

(CHUCKY enters all the way.)

CHUCKY: Don't have time for me today, huh? Well, hardy har har.

SHERIFF BART: Come on, Rosy. Let's go straighten this out with the Revrend.

(ROSY and SHERIFF BART exit.)

CHUCKY: Good to see you, Sheriff. (To FRANCIO) You know, I would like to shake the hand of the person who stole that Pecan.

FRANCIO: I was in bed by ten, baby.

CHUCKY: I mean, the bull semen heist seems like an amateurish prank in comparison to the raw havoc that missing Pecan has wrought upon this pathetic little town. I would bow down and grovel at the feet of the Pecan thief if I met him. You know what I mean?

FRANCIO: I know. Kiss his feet. If he had his toe nails done, I would probably kiss his feet too, baby.

CHUCKY: Freak. I gotta get outta here.

FRANCIO: You want a manicure, baby? A facial? I can pop those zits for jou.

(SONJA [Actor R] enters.)

SONJA: I'm baaaack. Can I help you?

CHUCKY: Yeah, put me down for a zit popping tomorrow at four. Later, girls. *(He exits.)*

FRANCIO: Don't take him serious.

SONJA: Everything okay while I was gone? Where did that lady go?

FRANCIO: Her daughter didn't want no facial. And I didn't do nothing.

SONJA: Okay, baby. Still no Mrs Bart?

*(MRS BART [Actor E] enters.)*

MRS BART: Here I am. Here I am. Sorry I'm late, girls. Oh, hello, uh, Francio. I didn't know—

FRANCIO: Thas all right.

SONJA: Francio, jer *permanente* will have to wait, okay? Cuz I got no Tammie right now.

FRANCIO: Thas all right, baby. I'll come back later.

SONJA: Come around five o'clock. I'll fix jou up *muy bonita.*

FRANCIO: Later, baby. *(He leaves.)*

SONJA: Later. Well, Mrs. Sheriff. Can you stand to have me instead of Tammie?

MRS BART: Actually, I would prefer to have you today. Apparently, Tammie has been seen driving a truck around town with a big, huge sign that says, "ED HAS THE PECAN, AND HE'S FROM OUTERSPACE."

SONJA: *Ay, dios mio.*

MRS BART: She is on the verge of some sort of breakdown. I almost didn't come today for fear she'd ruin my hair. I've heard she intends to drive that inflammatory sign through the parade.

SONJA: There must be some esplanation, Mrs Bart.

MRS BART: I have to look my best today, Sonja. I'm covering the Pecan Queen Pageant for the *Gazette* tonight…that is, assuming there still is a pageant—

(TAMMIE *[Actor T] throws the door open and stands in the middle of it. She is completely disheveled—torn clothing, dirt on her face and arms, hair like a rat's nest, a shotgun in hand, but she keeps an emphatically calm facade as if nothing were out of the ordinary. One senses she might burst like a cracked dam at any moment.*)

TAMMIE: Sorry I'm late, Sonja. Hello, Mrs Bart.

MRS BART & SONJA: *(Attempting cheerfulness)* Hello.

TAMMIE: I'm ready for your styling, Mrs Bart. Just give me one moment to collect my instruments.

MRS BART: Take your time, dear.

SONJA: No rush.

MRS BART: I'm actually having second thoughts about my hair today. In a bit of a hurry, you know.

TAMMIE: Now, Mrs Bart, I insist. Your hair is in a shambles.

(MRS BART *looks at* TAMMIE's *hair in bewilderment.*)

MRS BART: Is it?

TAMMIE: You just leave it to me. Today's a big day.

SONJA: Tammie, you okay, *chica?*

TAMMIE: Of course I'm okay…oh, you mean the shotgun. Haven't you ever heard of a shotgun wedding?

MRS BART: Uh—

TAMMIE: Me and Greeley. He'll be here soon. You'll see. He'll be looking for his truck, and when he gets here… *(She holds up the shotgun.)* We're getting married.

SONJA: Tammie, honey, this ain't the way to get a husband.

MRS BART: I'm afraid I'll have to be leaving—

TAMMIE: NOBODY LEAVES!!! *(Pumping the shotgun)* Today we're gonna have a wedding.

*(GREELEY [Actor G] enters. He doesn't immediately comprehend what's going on.)*

GREELEY: Where's my truck? Uh…hello? What's with the shotgun?

*(TAMMIE points the shotgun at GREELEY.)*

TAMMIE: Gitcher ass over here, Greeley! Mrs Bart, go fetch Revrend Pat.

MRS BART: Yes, of course.

TAMMIE: Sorry about yer appointment. We'll reschedule for tomorrow.

MRS BART: Not a problem, dear. First things first. *(She exits quickly.)*

GREELEY: My truck better be all right.

TAMMIE: Yer truck. Yer truck. Thas' all I hear about is yer truck. You do what I say today, or you'll never see that truck again. You understand, Greeley Green?

GREELEY: Yeah, I understand.

SONJA: *(Sitting down)* Go ahead, Greeley. Take a load off.

GREELEY: I have to go to the toilet.

TAMMIE: Yeah, fat chance.

GREELEY: I'm not lying. I have to go. I had Mexican for lunch. Look, if I don't come back, you can shoot Sonja.

SONJA: *Pendejo.*

TAMMIE: Yeah, okay, but I'm watching you.

(GREELEY *exits to the bathroom.*)

TAMMIE: There ain't any windows in there, right?

SONJA: No. *(Beat)* I hope it works out for you, Tammie, but it seems like a long shot to me.

TAMMIE: It's gonna work out.

(DIGGITY *[Actor G] sticks his head only in the front door.*)

DIGGITY: Sheriff Bart here yet?

TAMMIE: What? DIGGITY!

DIGGITY: Sheriff Bart here?

TAMMIE: No!

DIGGITY: You jes' wait 'til he gits here. Don't shoot anybody yet.

TAMMIE: Get the hell outta here, Diggity. Go get Revrend Pat.

(DIGGITY *exits.*)

TAMMIE: Damn ignoramus.

SONJA: He's got a little, tiny pencil dick.

TAMMIE: What???

SONJA: I heard.

*(Off stage, the voice of* SHERIFF BART *speaks through a megaphone.)*

SHERIFF BART: *(O S)* Okay, Tammie, we know yer in there.

TAMMIE: *(Going to the door and yelling out)* Yeah, okay, good. Now where's the Revrend?

SHERIFF BART: *(O S)* This is pointless, Tammie. I got three stations from the San Antonia news out here with cameras. You know I can't put the Revrend in harm's way. Yer gonna hafta let those hostages go.

TAMMIE: Ain't gonna happen Sheriff. One of two things will take place today. A bloodbath or a weddin'. You decide.

SHERIFF BART: *(O S)* Look, Tammie, the Revrend's on his way. Don't you go doin' anythang half cocked.

TAMMIE: Hey, Sheriff, I got a deal for you. You send that Revrend in here, and I'll tell you where the Great Pecan is hiding.

SHERIFF BART: *(O S)* Whudda you know about the Great Pecan, Tammie?

TAMMIE: I didn't take it, but I know who did. Have we got a deal? *(Towards the bathroom)* Greeley?

GREELEY: *(O S)* Tammie, you cain't rush these things.

TAMMIE: Have we got a deal, Sheriff?

SHERIFF BART: *(O S)* Why don't you send out Sonja?

SONJA: Oh no, no, no. I gotta see the end of this.

TAMMIE: No can do, Sheriff. She's a bridesmaid.

SONJA: Oh, Tammie! *Gracias!*

TAMMIE: Tell ya what, Sheriff, Sonja's in the wedding party. But I'll throw ya a bone… The Great Pecan is at Ed's house on 123 Bypass. He's using it in some kinda weird naked alien ritual deal.

*(GREELEY comes out of the bathroom.)*

GREELEY: Maybe I should talk to the Sheriff.

TAMMIE: YOU STAY PUT!!!

SHERIFF BART: *(O S)* Okay, Tammie, I'm sending my deputy to check out yer story. And now the Revrend's here. He's agreed to come in. Don't shoot him. I repeat: *do not shoot him.*

TAMMIE: Send him in.

GREELEY: I don't have a—a ring.

(TAMMIE *pulls out some keys on a ring.*)

TAMMIE: Here, we'll use this key ring.

GREELEY: Thas' ma spare set.

TAMMIE: Yep. How you think I got yer truck started? Got them out of yer glove compartment after I busted up yer window.

GREELEY: My—my window?

(REVEREND PAT *[Actor E] enters.*)

REVEREND PAT: Well, here I am. Let's get on with this. I've got a plane to catch. Duty calls in other ports. But I promised the Sheriff I'd do this before I depart. Are we all assembled?

TAMMIE: I'm just waitin' on my—

SHERIFF BART: *(O S)* Tammie, I got yer maid of honor out here!

TAMMIE: She's here! Send her in.

(*Enter* ROSY *[Actor R].* SONJA *snaps pictures.*)

ROSY: Sorry I'm late, Tammie.

TAMMIE: Rosy!

(ROSY *and* TAMMIE *both scream and hug.*)

TAMMIE: I'm finally gonna get married, honey!

ROSY: Hi Greeley.

GREELEY: Yeah, hi.

ROSY: Revrend Pat.

REVEREND PAT: *(To* ROSY*)* Well, well, well. *(To them all)* Let's do it before they send the SWAT team in.

GREELEY: Don't I get a maid of honor, uh, a best man?

TAMMIE: No!

GREELEY: I think I gotta go to the bathroom again.

TAMMIE: *(Waving the gun)* Get over here. There'll be plenty-uh time for that later.

REVEREND PAT: *(Nervous at the sight of the gun—rushing through)* Gather round then. Dearly beleaguered we are gathered here today to join these three in holy matrimoooony. Do you Greeley take this woman Rosy—

TAMMIE, ROSY & SONJA: —Tammie!

REVEREND PAT: Tam—Rose—Tammie to be yer lawful wedded wife to have and to hold 'til—'til—'til—

TAMMIE, ROSY & SONJA: —death!

REVEREND PAT: —death, I say, death, do you part?

GREELEY: Yeah, I mean, what choice do I have?

REVEREND PAT: Tammie, Tammie, do you take this man Reilley—

TAMMIE & ROSY:—Greeley!

REVEREND PAT: —Greeley, to be yer awful wedded husband, to have and to hold from this day forth 'til death [uh] do you part.

TAMMIE: I do.

ROSY: Oh!

REVEREND PAT: Then by the power vested in me, I now pronounce you man and wife. You may now kiss the bride. Mind the gun barrel.

*(TAMMIE kisses GREELEY. SONJA takes a picture and holds back the tears.)*

REVEREND PAT: Well, the time has come to say good-bye.

*(REVEREND PAT is about to leave, but then as a last thought, he dips ROSY into a kiss.)*

REVEREND PAT: Rosy, it could have been great in the Bahamas. *Adieu. (He exits.)*

TAMMIE: Yer truck is parked over at the El Burro restaurant round the back.

GREELEY: And it's okay?

TAMMIE: Except for a broken windshield, it's fine. I'll replace it.

GREELEY: If you wanted to get married this bad, why didn't you just say so?

TAMMIE: Greeley, I'm gonna strangle you.

SHERIFF BART: *(O S)* Tammie, Tammie, is everything all right in there? Sonja, Rosy, you okay?

ROSY & SONJA: Yeah, Sheriff.

SHERIFF BART: *(O S)* Look, Tammie, why don't you let me come in there? I think we can work this thang out. The media is gone. Sonja, you ain't gonna press no charges, right?

SONJA: Only if she don't throw the bouquet!

TAMMIE: Come on in, Sheriff.

*(SHERIFF BART [Actor E] enters—not nervous about the gun in the least.)*

SHERIFF BART: Everybody all right in here? You wanna give me that pea shooter, Tammie?

TAMMIE: It ain't loaded.

SHERIFF BART: I know it ain't, Missy.

*(DIGGITY [Actor G] sticks his head in the door.)*

DIGGITY: Sheriff? Sheriff Bart. Oh, hi Tammie. Congratulations on yer marriage. I bought you a toaster.

SHERIFF BART: What is it, Diggity?

DIGGITY: We got a pretty ugly situation over't Ed's house. That Rottweiler girl is leading an angry lynch mob over there now. They're callin' for the head of the man who stole the Great Pecan. The news stations from San Antonia are over there too. It's on the T V right now.

SHERIFF BART: Okay, round up everybody, and let's get over there pronto.

DIGGITY: Yes, Sheriff.

(DIGGITY *exits.* ROSY *makes her way over to the T V and turns it on—flipping stations.*)

SHERIFF BART: Tammie, I'm gonna trust you to come down to the station tomorrow. I'm gonna hafta come up with some kinda charges.

TAMMIE: I know, Sheriff.

SHERIFF BART: No more shenanigans for tonight.

GREELEY: Sheriff, what about me?

SHERIFF BART: You're free to go, Greeley. Congratulations on your marriage.

GREELEY: Congratulations...but...

(SHERIFF BART *exits in a hurry. On the television, all pre-taped on video—though it could be done live in some sort of mock T V frame—*PRISCILLA *is speaking to a newscaster.*)

SONJA: Look, it's on the T V.

(*On the T V,* KITTY ST CLAIR)

KITTY ST CLAIR: (*On T V*) Thank you, Bill, we are out here on 123 Bypass outside the barn of a man known in Seguin only as "Ed." Apparently, we have no last name for him. This Ed is holed up inside the barn, and an angry crowd is starting to gather with calls of "string him up," and "dirty pecan thief," and "I've got a rope in my truck." If you want to put a human face on the kind of pain this man has cause by allegedly stealing the Great Pecan, you need go no further than high school senior, Priscilla Rottweiller.

(PRISCILLA *steps aggressively into the camera.*)

SONJA: She should have got a make over.

PRISCILLA: I'm here to represent all of the young girls who won't be able to compete for Pecan Queen this year because of this evil man. He deserves the strictest punishment our law allows. Now that we've caught him, and now that justice *will* prevail, perhaps after time and intense therapy the wounds may heal.

KITTY ST CLAIR: *(On T V)* Well, there you have it, Bill, this angry mob is ready to explode at any moment...

(*There is a loud explosion, almost like a rocket ignition. The barn collapses.*)

KITTY ST CLAIR: *(On T V)* Wait, what's that? Oh my gosh, it looks like the barn's just exploded. Did you get that?

ROSY: Oh dear Lord.

GREELEY: ED!

CHUCKY: *(On T V)* I blew it up! I did it! Free the space man! Don't put him in a test tube! FREEEEEEDOM!

(*ROSY goes over to look out the window.*)

KITTY ST CLAIR: *(On T V)* Sorry, Bill, there are some bad apples in the crowd.

(*There is an otherworldy sound.*)

KITTY ST CLAIR: *(On T V)* Oh dear Lord, rising from the rubble, Bill, are you seeing this? It looks like some, some kind of aircraft, or space craft...oh Sweet Jesus... hovering—just hovering in the sky. Tell me you are getting this!

(GREELEY, ROSY, SONJA *and* TAMMIE *are all about to go
outside. Cut to stock footage of space ship, then the T V.
goes blank for a second before* ED *comes on the screen. He is
speaking from his spaceship. They all stop in their tracks.*)

ED: Greetings earthlings and Texans.

ROSY: Oh my Lord.

TAMMIE: I told ya he was an alien!

ED: I thought our mutual coexistence was an
experiment that could work. Your planet has a wealth
of the valuable *pecan*, which we use on our world for
fuel, sustenance, and tanning oil.

GREELEY: *(Forlorn)* Ed!

ED: I admit I crossed the boundries of proper
intergalactic etiquette when I took your sacred shrine.
I saw it falling into disrepair, saw the grey rat-birds
leave the liquidy white excrement upon it, saw the
young pubescent beings spray it with ozone damaging
methylene chloride based dyes. I thought you had
forsaken your sacred icon.

SONJA: It's true, the T V does add ten pounds.

ED: I was not prepared for the mosaic of beautiful
human emotions at its disappearance. I saw the pecan
as a product for profitable resale on my world and not
as the spiritual, mystical beacon which your people
obviously believe it to be. Therefore, I am returning the
Great Pecan to you with my sincerest apologies.

ROSY: Oh thank Jesus! The Festival is saved!

ED: I dare not make another landing lest I incur your
further ire, but I will now release the Great Pecan with
a parachute to fetter its descent. With sorrow I take my
leave of you, and I particularly will miss the one called
Greeley—

GREELEY: Ed!

ED: —who was a good friend. In the language of my people...*preHHHHa brrreej Greeley-neeshhh.* Until we meet again.

*(The T V goes blank.)*

ROSY: It ain't workin' anymore.

SONJA: Let's try the radio.

*(SONJA turns on the radio. They all crowd around.)*

JOHNNY JOHNS: *(V O)* —can all see the Great Pecan now as it glides down to the earth. It looks like it's headed toward 123 Bypass. Police and State Troopers have cleared off the highways... Oh, wait, there's one lone car on the highway who's apparently broken through the police barrier. It appears to be a purple B M W. He does not see the descending Pecan, and, oh my God, they appear to be on a direct collision course. Somebody's got to stop that car. *(Overlapping)* He just doesn't seem to realize what's been going on.

ROSY: *(Overlapping)* Oh dear Lord, I still love him...

*(ROSY and TAMMIE hug.)*

JOHNNY JOHNS: *(V O)* Oh! Oh my! He's been hit.

*(ROSY gasps.)*

OHNNY JOHNS: *(V O)* He's been hit by the Great Pecan! The car has been literally squashed by the great weight of the Pecan. If anyone is alive in there, it would be a miracle...a miracle.

ROSY: I can't take it.

JOHNNY JOHNS: *(V O)* We're now being told that the car belongs to Revrend Pat of the Third Baptist Church. The police are racing toward him now. If you're just joining us, an alien spaceship just dropped the Great Pecan out of the sky, and it has landed on Revrend Pat of the Third Baptist Church. There's Sheriff Bart now. He's looking inside the car.

ROSY: Oh, for the love of God!

JOHNNY JOHNS: *(V O)* He's giving us the thumbs up! I say he's giving us the thumbs up.

(ROSY, SONJA *and* TAMMIE *cheer.* GREELEY *could take it or leave it.*)

JOHNNY JOHNS: *(V O)* I'm quite sure the jaws of life will be needed to excavate the Revrend from the wreckage, but at least we know that he's alive.

ROSY: Thank you, Jesus.

JOHNNY JOHNS: *(V O)* This is Johnny Johns. This has been the noon traffic report. *(Beat)* Okay, let's switch gears here a little. We gotta send a big ole congratulations to Tammie Lynn Schneider and Greeley Green who finally tied the knot. They were married today in a private ceremony over't Sonja's Beauty Parlor. They're registered over't Horner's Department store if you want to send a gift.

GREELEY: We're registered?!

JOHNNY JOHNS: *(V O)* This next song goes out to Mister and Mrs Greeley Green. All the best y'all.

*(A country song plays on the radio.)*

ROSY: Scuse me. I'll just go freshen up.

SONJA: Don't mind me.

(ROSY *exits to bathroom.* SONJA *gives the couple some space.*)

TAMMIE: Shall we go get your truck, Greeley?

GREELEY: I don't know what the hell is going on today.

TAMMIE: You wanna go to the Dixie Drive-In tonight? I think there's a double feature: *Mad Max Beyond Thunderdome* and *E T*.

GREELEY: Yeah, okay.

TAMMIE: Can we bring Rosy along? She's in mourning for the Revrend.

GREELEY: He didn't die.

TAMMIE: Yeah, well he's dead to this town.

GREELEY: Yeah, sure, she can come. *(Quietly, to the heavens)* Ed...

TAMMIE: Here's yer spare set of keys.

GREELEY: Uh, tha's all right. You keep 'em.

TAMMIE: Really?

GREELEY: Yeah, what the hell. You can drive it if you want.

*(TAMMIE is choked up by the gesture. That's all she ever wanted.)*

TAMMIE: I don't really wanna drive it.

GREELEY: What the hell did you steal it for?

TAMMIE: I just wanted you to make the offer.

GREELEY: I WILL NEVER UNDERSTAND WOMEN!

TAMMIE: I love you, Greeley Green.

GREELEY: Yeah, well, I love you too, honey pie.

*(GREELEY and TAMMIE kiss. ROSY comes to the door and watches them as they dance the Texas Two Step. Lights fade slowly to black.)*

*(End of large cast version of the last scene)*

### END OF PLAY

# AUTHOR'S NOTES

## CONCERNING THE CHARACTERS AND THE ACTORS

For the four actor version of the play, I attempted to be as kind as possible to the actors in the quick change department, but sometimes a change needs to take place in the course of a blackout. If it can be pulled off successfully, it will not only keep the play moving along, but it will offer some fun for the audience and a challenge for the actors. I recommend layering clothes in those instances and designing simple representative costumes that can be pulled off in seconds. Watch the N B A players as they enter a basketball game and rip off their warm ups. Sometimes a character just sticks his head in the door, so maybe you can get away with just a hat.

The last scene as written for four actors will require some practice. I know as an actor myself how such technical worries can suck a lot of concentration away from performance, so please be kind to your actors and schedule rehearsals to practice the changes. In the last scene I wanted to pay homage to the French farces where there are a lot of people coming in and out of slamming doors, but with a slight variation—practically every character in the play (fourteen of them anyway) enters the last scene, and of course, each character is played by four actors, so the character/

costume change becomes a sort of "slamming door" itself.

## CONCERNING THE SETS

Sets can be representative and simple.

## CONCERNING THE VIDEO

In the New York City production we found some footage of a barn being pulled down *(it looked like it exploded)*, and we found a 3D model of a spaceship, which we animated with a program called Poser. We had the actors perform in front of a green screen and merged all the footage. But if you don't have clever video folks at your disposal, think Ed Wood. Do something creative and cheesy, or simply have Kitty refer to the explosion and the space ship which is just off screen. It is fun for the audience to see it if you can pull it off.

## CONCERNING THE MUSIC

I'd love for the real 1980s country music of Candee Land to be used. She is really from Seguin, Texas. Her music is hard to track down. Hopefully at the time of publication there will be a music licensing option attached to the play licensing option. If you don't see that and want to know more about how to license Candee's music for your production, email Broadway Play Publishing Inc. Alternately my current contact information can always be found on my website, www.StephenBittrich.com.

## SEGUIN IS A REAL PLACE

Some of the ideas in the play are based on truth, but most of it really isn't true. Truth is often too unbelievable. None of the characters are real people, but some are based on parts of people I've known or heard about.

The setting of this play, Seguin, Texas, is a real town in south Texas, where I grew up. There really is a Great Pecan, a huge concrete statue (or is it real?) right near the Court House. People in Seguin don't really pay much mind to the Pecan these days, but I like to go visit it whenever I'm in town. It's not like the *Mona Lisa*, you can walk right up and touch it.

We say "Puh *kahn*" in Seguin. I noticed people in New York City say "*Pee* kan," and I always had a notion they said it that way thinking that's how we say it in the south. Well, we don't. At least not in Seguin, Texas.

The Great Pecan, thankfully, has never been stolen, but I do refer to a bull semen heist in the script. That did happen. I have a newspaper clipping from the *Seguin Gazette* (unfortunately with no date) which reads "BULL SEMEN MISSING: Guadalupe County sheriff's officers are investigating the theft of $4,000 worth of bull semen and other property stolen from a farm in the Marion area. Deputy Robert E. Murphy was called to the Schertz Animal Clinic Wednesday where he met with Dr. Kermit Harborth, a veterinarian. Harborth said there had been a series of break-ins at his farm on Weil Road in the Marion area. A cattle blower valued at $289 was discovered missing on Feb. 6, and a pair of Showmaster variable-speed clippers valued at $200 apparently were taken on Feb. 10 or Feb. 11, Harborth told the deputy. On Wednesday, he discovered that a semen tank containing more than $4,000 worth of registered and syndicated cattle semen was missing along with a liquid nitrogen tank. Chief Investigator Larry Morawietz said the Texas Rangers have been contacted and are assisting in the investigation."

The idea for a shotgun wedding in a beauty parlor is based on truth also, but in Florida, not Texas. Here's an excerpt from *Jet* magazine, June 22, 1992, Page 19: "MARRY ME! William E. Young, 44, of Cape Coral,

Fla., really wanted to get married, but Bonnie Ribich, 43, had broken off their engagement. Young would not be denied, and walked into a beauty salon with a shotgun and held Ribich hostage for five hours, demanding that police send in a minister to marry them. More than 40 officers surrounded the building until Young surrendered and was charged with false imprisonment and aggravated assault."

The formula Reverend Pat devised for people to figure out how much money they should tithe was from a real televangelist I saw on the T V. I more or less copied that formula verbatim: "Have ya got a figure? Now I want you ta take that figure, and I want you ta double it—right now—I want you ta double it! Then I want you ta double it again!!"

After I finished the play, I wondered if it would ever be put on in my hometown, and I wondered who it would offend. Those who think I'm making fun of the Great Pecan? Those who think I'm making fun of the church? Or worst perhaps, those who think I'm making fun of Texas. I hope I offend none of these. It's a only a comedy, written with great affection and dedicated to the place where I happily grew up, Home of the Great Pecan.

CHARACTER BREAKDOWN
FOR 4 PERSON CASTING:

ACTOR G
Greeley Green
Deputy Diggity
Deke Rottweiler
Johnny Johns (voice only)
Francio
Les Glenehinkel

ACTOR E
Ed
Sheriff Bart
Reverend Pat
Billy Pomgranite *(voice only)*
Mrs Bart
Orest Stelmach

ACTOR T
Tammie Lynn Schneider
Mrs Rottweiler
Chucky Connors
Kitty St Clair, Newscaster *(on video only)*

ACTOR R
Rosy Stadtmueller
Priscilla Rottweiler
Sonja Guarez

## LIST OF SETS

1 Ed's back porch (I:1, I:8, II:1)
2 Tammie Lynn's back porch (I:2)
3 Sheriff Bart's office (I:3, I:7)
4 The Baptist Church (I:4)
5 Outside the Baptist Church (I:5)
6 Reverend Pat's church office (I:5, II:3)
7 Bathroom of Priscilla Rottweiler (I:6, II:2)
8 Beauty parlor of Sonja Guarez (I:9, II:5)
9 Glenehinkel's hardware store (II:4)

## BIBLE REFERENCES

Romans 13:14
Corinthians I 7:2
Matthew 18:8
Matthew 6:19-20
Matthew 19:24
2 Samuel 11:2
James 1:13
Proverbs 6:27
Matthew 5:28
Ephesians 2:1-8
Leviticus 19:34
Deuteronomy 14:21-26